# UPWARD

## From Sin, Through Grace, to Glory.

"FOR ME TO LIVE IS CHRIST AND TO DIE IS GAIN."

BY

REV. B. B. HOTCHKIN.

PHILADELPHIA:
PRESBYTERIAN PUBLICATION COMMITTEE,
1334 CHESTNUT STREET.
NEW YORK: A. D. F. RANDOLPH, 770 BROADWAY.

Westcott & Thomson,
Stereotypers, Philada.

# PREFATORY NOTE.

This little book is meant to reflect the dealings of God with the heart of his child; in other words, to be a book of Christian experience.

The holy activities of the age will never displace this truth, that the Christian draws his *abiding* comforts from the religion of his heart. To assure himself of those comforts, he needs often to turn aside from the sympathetic influences of the outward religious movements, and find himself alone with God. There he may ask himself how much of what he calls his religion *is* religion; how much of it is born of the people, and how much of God; how much would abide, and how much perish, with the dying away of the public stir. In this dealing with the vitalities of religion there is found the strongest incitement to its public activities, and the true secret of patient perseverance in such activities.

So far as the subject of these pages is concerned, no apology is needed. Reasons enough exist why Christian experience should remain one of the standing topics of religious literature.

# CONTENTS.

I.

PAGE

Reconciliation with God. First—The Longing..... 9

II.

Reconciliation with God. Second—The Accomplishment........................................ 28

III.

Conscience. First—At War................................ 42

IV.

Conscience. Second—At Peace.............................. 50

V.

PAGE

The Victory that Overcometh the World. First —The Reliance.... 59

VI.

The Victory that Overcometh the World. Second —Endurance.... 70

VII.

Assurance. First—A Lawful Expectation.... 80

VIII.

Assurance. Second—The Witness of the Spirit.... 97

IX.

Love. First—The Chief Grace.... 110

X.

Love. Second—Its Scope.... 124

XI.

The Service of Doing. First—Incitements.... 137

XII.

PAGE

THE SERVICE OF DOING. Second—Encouragements... 155

XIII.

THE SERVICE OF DOING. Third—Fruit.................. 169

XIV.

THE SERVICE OF SUFFERING. First—The Consecration and the Covenant.............................................. 182

XV.

THE SERVICE OF SUFFERING. Second—The Submission of Faith................................................... 193

XVI.

THE SERVICE OF SUFFERING. Third—Christ Sustaining and Forearming........................................ 205

XVII.

THE BORDER LAND. First—Reassurance.................. 221

XVIII.

THE BORDER LAND. Second—The Gloom and the Light. 238

## XIX.

PAGE
THE BORDER LAND. Third—The Covenant Slumber. 248

## XX.

HEAVEN. First—Things which Eye hath not seen nor Ear heard.................................................... 262

## XXI.

HEAVEN. Second—The Everlasting Sabbath............. 278

# UPWARD.

## I.

### RECONCILIATION WITH GOD.

#### FIRST—THE LONGING.

THE first word spoken by a sinner on earth to his God expresses the true terror of the unforgiven soul: "I heard thy voice in the garden, and I was afraid." This awful fear of the presence of his Maker arose from his consciousness of an unsettled wrong then lying between himself and God. The voice from which he shrank was the same which he had often before heard, not only without dread, but with unspeakable delight. But then it was the voice of his heavenly Father and Friend. His relations with that Being were unbroken; he knew that between himself and his Sovereign all was right, and, consequently, all was peaceful. He had no unhappy fear of God, for the love which was shed abroad in his heart, and which prompted his obedience, made the life which he lived like an angel's life—the life of love. Where this holy affection dwells terror has no home.

Yes, in confidence and love it *was* an angel's life. Up now with our thoughts to that life!—to the dwelling-place of the sinless beings who do ever behold the face of our Father which is in heaven!

By contrast, the contemplation will afford the most impressive view of the weariness of abiding under the sense of unforgiven sin. Through it we shall better understand both the occasion and the character of the unreconciled sinner's pantings for rest.

Celestial ones, angelic and glorified,

draw near to the throne upon which their *infinitely holy Sovereign* sits. His holiness awakens no dread in them, because it involves them in no condemnation. It ensures their happiness, and not their ruin. While its intrinsic beauty, rendering it worthy of love from all worlds, becomes for them a delightful contemplation, they know that its bearing toward themselves is never wrath, but always love.

They adore the *might* of God. Their songs address Him that sitteth upon the throne—the emblem of dominion and power. From his arm of strength they have nothing to fear. Over them it is extended with protecting vigilance. When it is raised in destructive power, it falls only upon the enemies of heaven.

Their anthems celebrate the *righteousness* of the eternal Lawgiver. The same scrupulous justice which ensures wrath for sin, makes the pleasure of obedience doubly blessed, because, in addition to its intrinsic joy, there comes the assurance of an approving reward.

With glowing hearts they contemplate the sublime structure of the *government of God*, immeasurable in magnitude and infinite in wisdom. Before their view is spread a system of polity embracing the universe for its field and eternity for its length of administration; infinitely comprehensive, and just as infinitely minute; a subject for eternal study and unutterable wonder. Contemplating the far-reaching plans and sure faithfulness of this administration, they feel no alarm from the truth, so terrible to souls in revolt, that this government has a special bearing upon each individual, from which no power can deliver and which no flight can escape. They never tremble under the thought of the omniscience of the Sovereign in this dominion. For them there is no dismay in the inquiry, "Whither shall I go from thy Spirit, or whither shall I flee from thy presence?"—no fearfulness in the reflection that if they ascend into heaven, or make their beds in hell, or take the wings of the morning and dwell in the uttermost parts of the sea, the eye of the holy God will follow them, and his arm will bring them forth. All which makes this government fearful to the wicked commends it to the good. The same principles which doom the one, exalt the other.

But happier, as we may suppose, than all else in the experience of these shining ones, they live in the light of the *love of God.* Beauty loves the light; it is only deformity that dreads exposure. Those dwellers in the everlasting light of the love of God look abroad without fear, for the miscreant features of sin do not clothe their faces with shame. They look upward without dread, for those rays are shed with *conforming* power upon themselves. Love, holy, celestial love, is chief in that glory of the Lord which, reflected as in a glass upon him whose faith beholds it, changes him into the same image from glory to glory.

Now reverse all these emotions, and we have the experience of the unreconciled sinner. He is terrified by the Presence before which seraphs rejoice. Like him who was afraid when he heard the voice of the Lord God walking in the garden in the cool of the day, his soul is troubled by the entire loss of the divine conformity. If he dares to think of the holiness of God, he beholds in it the condemnation of himself. There is some strange arrangement in his powers of observation which ever forbids him to contemplate God's moral attributes by themselves alone. In the same picture where he gazes on the divine holiness, that loathsome thing, his own heart, always occupies a conspicuous place. It is one of the weary experiences of impenitency that the sinner, in all his moral contemplations, is compelled to meet this double vision, God and his own heart side by side. And thus the delight with which a world of holy beings view the righteousness, the holiness and the love of God, becomes in him terror whenever he turns his eye toward the same glorious spectacle.

Some of the most terrible convictions of sin are produced by a sight of the glory of God. The vision once overwhelmed even a good man, whose spirit was yet too far short of heaven to bear the view of the Lord on his throne, high and lifted up, his train filling the temple, the seraphim standing above and crying one to another, "Holy, holy is the Lord of hosts; the whole earth is full of his glory!" It was the contrast between this awful majesty and his own sinful person which unmanned him. "Then, said I, Woe is me, for I am undone, because I am a man of unclean lips, and I dwell in the midst of a people of unclean lips; for mine eyes have seen the King, the Lord of hosts." If one whose soul had felt the peace of forgiving love was thus bowed with shame on beholding himself in direct contrast with God, is there any wonder that the sinner shrinks with affright from a similar exhibition? In this part of his experience he knows the truth that there is no peace for the wicked. Here he recognizes that first insuppressable want of the unforgiven soul—the want of reconciliation with God.

Terror in view of the natural greatness of God may not be so instantly felt. Men of no religion find some points of observation where they become inspired with noble thoughts of the divine grandeur, and they have recorded such thoughts in language which will live in the memorials of human eloquence. They have studied the course of the divine administration as we peruse the histories of empires or the revelations of science, and, surprised by the skill of the system and the strength of its working, they have frankly and admiringly confessed its author God. In the book of nature they have read the beauty and sublimity of his ways. They have looked on summer landscapes when their dews sparkled in the morning sun, and they have spoken of the creating and adorning hand in words of rapture. They have trod the rustic lawn,

> "Where violets sweet
> Purpled the moss-bed at their feet,"

and thought of the wondrous transformation of ashy dust into manifold shapes and colors of beauty. They have gazed upon cataracts whose roar has been the cradle-hymn of infant centuries and the death-song of old expiring ages; they have followed the Eternal footsteps along the paths of astronomical science, and there beheld Him "who spreadeth out the heavens, and treadeth upon the waves of the sea; who maketh Arcturus, Orion and Pleiades, and the chambers of the south," until among these exhaustless fields of wonder they have repeated with real enthusiasm, "O Lord, how manifold are thy works! in wisdom hast thou made them all."

But even here, among these spectacles of the natural greatness of God, the sinner is troubled if he looks too far. The field is sublime, but his view can take no broad sweep of it without lighting upon points in the Divine majesty of which he dare not think. He fears to reflect that the attributes disclosed exist for the support of that moral government to which he is inseparably linked. The great thought of infinite strength burdens the soul that is compelled to contemplate it as the power of an unreconciled and avenging God. The Divine omniscience which, in the abstract, he has often admired, becomes terrible under the reflection that this all-seeing Eye is searching him through, and that an escape from its scrutiny is hopeless. When for an instant his imagination glows with the lofty conception of God measuring the waters in the hollow of his hand, meting out heaven with the span, comprehending the dust of the earth in a measure, weighing the mountains in scales and the hills in a balance, stretching out the heavens as a curtain, and spreading them out as a tent to dwell in, how soon this enthusiasm is chilled by the suggestion of conscience that it is not for him to say,

> "This awful God is mine—
> My Father and my love!"

In short, his Maker has no perfection which he can behold without dread. From the divine *holiness* conviction of sin flashes upon his conscience and wears down his soul. From the *greatness* of the Eternal terrific apprehensions of wrath arise. Thus remorse and fear divide the dominion within him. Sinner, Jesus knew you better than you know yourself when he spoke of you as weary and heavy-laden. Better than yourself he knew your first spiritual want when he offered you rest.

But some sinners, without really meaning to be uncandid, tell us that these representations do not accord with their personal experience. They speak of hours and days spent in mirth; some refer to their constitutional tranquillity of temper, and others to their habitual joviality; and they array this experience against the testimony that a life of sin is *always* miserable—that "the wicked man travaileth with pain *all his days*." Some go farther, and insist that even from a scriptural stand-point we must expect to see carnal ease the more frequent type of impenitency; that with "the harp and the viol, the tabret and pipe and wine in their feasts, they regard not the work of the

Lord;" that the life of the sinner, being that of one who has *no fear of God* before his eyes, is more likely to be spent in spiritual stupidity than in terror. Such views have an air of candor, and should be candidly considered.

Let it be admitted that the general course of sin is one of stolid indifference to religion; that under the protection of this apathy the sinner in the hot pursuit of worldly good can hold remorse and alarm at bay; that substituting the shrines of pleasure, fame or gold for the altar's heavenly worship, he can paganize his nobler nature, and, forgetting there is a God above, he can also forget that he lives an unforgiven rebel under his dominion. The necessity for admitting the reality of this experience is, alas! too imperative. It is too true that the sinner is often reckless of the fear as well as the claims of God.

But does this prove that there is ever a

moment of tranquillity of heart in a life of sin? Let it be granted that the Bible does sustain the sinner's assertion that he is able to regard the most solemn things with apathy: are we to admit the wild inference that recklessness is peace, or that because his impenitency does not impress his moral feelings, therefore it does not *trouble* him? What if it is said that there is no fear of God before the sinner's eyes? In the same discourse, and in immediate connection, it is recorded: "Destruction and *misery* are in their ways, *and the way of peace have they not known.*" Both these statements are true, and there is no difficulty in reconciling them. We have a witness already on the stand, one that the sinner has himself called up—his own experience. Pushing the examination of that witness, we may find that there is a false face to be torn from spiritual carelessness, and that the sentence of God—*no peace to the wicked*—is an eternal inscription cut into the monument of living humanity to record the death of holiness in the human heart.

From that witness we wring out this confession—reluctant, slow, but terrible—*the sinner purchases his carelessness at the expense of his moral degradation.* He must forget his immortal nature and lose sight of this noblest fact in his existence, that he is a being of superior order, associated by filiation with the nature of God. Every moment of exemption from terror of the Divine anger is a moment of practical atheism—"without God in the world." He does not say, "I contemplate my relation to the character, law and government of God, and then I am at peace." But he parries remorse and fear by cultivating obliviousness of his relation to his heavenly Sovereign. He looks abroad upon earth for comfort because he dares not look up to heaven. He pants in the chase after groveling pleasures because the cessation of this pursuit leaves time for solemn reflection, and reflection gives conscience an opportunity to speak. Every observation of the order of nature tells him that he looks in the wrong direction for good. Nature teaches that the fountain is the place from whence to seek supplies—that those who desire good should come to the exhaustless treasure of goodness. The most simple principles of order instruct him that an immortal soul will yearn for immortal joys, and that the attempt to satiate these cravings with the trifles of an hour is only an effort to wipe out from the soul the imprint of the Divinity and shrivel it to the capacity of the brute.

The intelligent sinner is not ignorant of this; why, then, does he not follow the suggestions of this plain order of things? He wants pleasure; why does he not go at once to the fountain of pleasure? He longs for good; why does he not seek it direct from the exhaustless treasure? The natural yearnings of the soul prompt her to fly to some boundless field of enjoyment; why not bid her plume herself for a flight to realms of glory and honor and immortality in pursuit of the everlasting life? Why will he clip her soaring pinions and force her to forget her heavenly birth by fastening her as a crawling worm to the dirt? Why in his search for delights will he thus repudiate his own judgment, browbeat his immortality, and condemn his spiritual nature to chafe in sensual fetters until its noble aspirations are all dead?

The same monotonous answer is ever at hand. His soul is oppressed with a consciousness of unreconciliation toward God, and he is afraid to look heavenward for a single blessing. He dares not attempt the pursuit of any good when the attempt involves an effort to approach God. He remembers the wrong which lies between his soul and God; he must seek an escape from the remorse which a sense of that wrong awakens, and so he flies to his carnal delights to become oblivious of all that he ought to remember.

Yet he finds, after all, that the sea of worldly delights is not filled with the true Lethean waters. Its power to produce oblivion is but temporary, existing only during the moments of actual immersion. Hence he must plunge again and again. In other words, the frolic, revel, or more refined social gayeties, the mirage of human ambition, the golden will-of-the-wisp—some of these must be pursued incessantly, for they form the only carnal relief for the pain of solemn reflections upon his relations to God. And then, forsooth, the *pleasures* to which he is driven and held by such terrors are cited in proof that a life of impenitency is not a life of pain!

Lord, deliver us from sin! Deliver our

consciences from its burden and our hearts from its pollution! And in special mercy, O Lord! deliver our reason from its logic!

The truth is, all forgetfulness of God which is secured by such means, so far from being a *medicine* for the sinner's burning moral fever, is only a *symptom* of its existence. The search for relief proves the reality of the anguish. The fact of this apathy toward religion must be considered in connection with its nature and the manner in which it is produced. The very recklessness of the sinner, when we reflect how and why it is cultivated, is one of the strongest confirmations of the word: "Trouble and anguish shall make him afraid."

There lies in every moral nature a sense that the short and sure road to peace is reconciliation with God who has been disowned, and his government which has been cast off.

# II.

## RECONCILIATION WITH GOD.

### SECOND—THE ACCOMPLISHMENT.

THE time has come for the unreconciled sinner to turn from this wearisome strife and seek his peace with God by the *cross of Christ.* "All things are of God, who hath reconciled us to himself by Jesus Christ."

But what is this cross of Christ? In fact and efficacy it is this:

When sin had done its worst upon human character and condition, the Divine arrangement for mercy was revealed. Its execution began in "the blood of Christ, who, through the Eternal Spirit, offered himself without spot to God." Sin was enthroned in a corrupt nature. This corruption, derived from the common source of human generation, was universal, and it pervaded the whole human nature. The conscience must be purged from dead works, and the whole man washed from moral loathsomeness. So also the amenability of the sinner to the highest claims and extremest penalty of the holy law of heaven must be met, honored and satisfied.

The greatness of the sacrifice was commensurate with the great demand. The Redeemer met the case as he found it. His sacrifice was real, for he made *his soul an offering for sin.* In this work he stood in the sinner's place; for, all sinless himself, God *made him to be sin for us.* It is not in outward sufferings alone that the final doom of the unforgiven sinner consists. Its chief element is the frown of God felt *in the soul* as a burden of wrath. Let whoever doubts this, read Revelation vi. 16, 17. This *soul-felt* wrath of God was the cup which Jesus drank to the dregs. From his cross we hear little complaint of physical sufferings, terrible as they were. The thorns in his brow and the nails in his flesh awoke, so far as we learn, no cry of anguish. That dying expostulation, whose echoes will linger for ever through the realm of redemption, was pressed from the soul of this sinless One by the weight of this great wrath—a feeling of desertion, as if in anger forsaken by God.

It is vain to ask how this could be felt at the moment of his most intense obedience to the will of God, and when he must have known that the Father was well-pleased with it all. Redemption is the *great mystery of godliness.* We do not study it as cold philosophers, nor ask for scientific solutions of its problems; for the sweetest element in religion will be gone when proud men have outridden all faith with their philosophy. We stand in the shadow of the cross, where the very ground is tremulous under the quiverings of the sufferer. We long for redemption from such wrath as the soul feels when, deserted in anger, it looks in vain for one smile of God. We listen, and, lo! that shriek, with which our voices should have rent the prison of despair—"*My God! my God! why hast thou forsaken me?*"

There, for the moment, that was endured which the law doomed us to endure for ever. There the chastisement of our peace was once upon Christ, and now his heavenly intercession preserves for that atonement an ever-living efficacy. Thus we learn that, as our sin wrought his death, so his righteousness can work our life—that as he was made sin for us, so we are made the righteousness of God in him. This may be all dark to those who would straiten the Divine ways to the scant limits of human understanding, but it is enough for us that we behold the beauty of the scheme in the light of our wants.

It is the provision that we need, and before we are moved from this faith, we must hear some better answer to the great question, "How should man be just with God?"

Still the way to reconciliation with God through Christ is not fully disclosed until we are told of the Holy Spirit following, with his peculiar influences, the work of Christ in the world. Every solemn emotion in which the sinner is reminded of his need of redeeming mercy is the whisper of that Spirit in his soul. Every loud, open call, through providential dispensations or the messages of grace, is the same warning of God. When he turns from his revolt, it is because the Spirit works in him repentance and submission. When he is justified, he feels the power of the same Spirit imparting to him believing faith and applying to him the pardon purchased in the atonement. Under all the remaining experience of religion this Spirit upholds him in the hour of temptation, strengthens his heart for duty, attends him with its support in the furnace of affliction, sustains him in the hour of death, and makes safe his passage to glory.

This, then, is the cross of Christ. This is the power, and these are the blessings which well out from the atonement, their spring.

Here, too, arises another and crowning view of sin. A wholesome estimate of sin is ever the accompaniment of reconciliation with God. The dreadfulness of human rebellion must be measured by the greatness of the sacrifice indispensable for the change of the rebel to a loving subject of the throne of heaven. The Lord Jesus stooped no lower and endured no more than was demanded by the magnitude of the guilt of man. The sight of our suffering Saviour also gives this darker aspect to the soul's revolt—that it is pursued after conditions of peace are opened and the sinner's reconciliation is besought on the gentlest terms. For now his revolt carries all the appearance of a desperate purpose on his part to try the issue—who shall triumph, himself or God—whether he shall dethrone his Maker or be crushed by Omnipotence.

But, above all other aspects of sin, it appears most shocking in view of the *love* of the cross. There the Redeemer of sinners meets his hour of agony without even the consolation of his Father's smile. Let us draw near to this great sight, that we may know how God feels for men. The sufferer seems to ask if there be any sorrow like unto his sorrow. What a mingling of horror of sin and tenderness for the sinner in that appeal from his cross, unspoken in words, but coming out from the mute anguish in his eye: "*The cup of wrath! I drink it to save you from drinking it for ever. My heart of love! behold its choicest compassions lavished on yourself: shall it not win the recompense of your love?*

Is it not enough that the rebel has revolted from his Maker, broken the righteous covenant and placed himself in the way of the terrors of the Almighty? Will not love now subdue the heart which every other excellence of God has failed to move? The matchless love of his injured Sovereign, expressed in the unexampled sorrow of Christ on the cross—can he withstand that also?

Heaven and earth, hear and be astonished! The proud rebel has not even the grace to *deplore* his own part in loading the Redeemer with this affliction. He cares nothing for the share which his own sins have borne in the deed. He bestows perhaps one cold look upon the solemn spectacle—perhaps turns his ear for one callous hearing of the imploring entreaty of Christ—then bids the tender Spirit of grace begone, and exults that he is above the subduing influence of the compassion of Heaven. Who will now doubt the deep, the *radical* depravity of the human heart?

Extend the view to that field of the holy Spirit's operations which has been noticed, and the madness of this rebellion takes the suicidal type. In sinning against the Holy Ghost the sinner sins against his own soul. That Spirit is the last agent ever to be employed in restoring rebels to the favor of God. Hence the necessary consequence of resisting its motions in the heart is the self-exclusion of the sinner from the hope of reconciliation. Only in this light can we comprehend the import of the woe which God denounces upon those from whom he departs.

This, then, is sin in the light of the redeeming mercy—the sinner as seen from the stand-point of Calvary. The unhappy creature who shrinks from looking over the smallest of his accounts with God can yet do this. He can tread under foot the

Son of God, count the blood of the covenant wherewith he was sanctified an unholy thing, and do despite to the Spirit of grace. If he does not carry it to the irrevocable point where God finally gives him over to himself, he will be led by this convicting power of the cross to yield himself a captive to grace. Why did he not long since do it? The only answer is found in the insanity of human rebellion against God. The last battle is often the fiercest. Sometimes the very malignancy of the final struggle shows to the combatant what a heart he possesses, and leads him, under a Divine enabling, to the great resolve that such a heart cannot be endured, and it shall submit. At the feet of Jesus, "clothed and in his right mind," the penitent and restored soul sings of the reconciling grace—

"I heard the voice of Jesus say,
Come unto me and rest;
Lay down, thou weary one, lay down
Thy head upon my breast.

> "I came to Jesus as I was,
> Weary, and worn, and sad;
> I found in him a resting-place,
> And he has made me glad."

Here is the first unterrified view of God. The sinner has turned from the strife in which he knew that he was wrong, and surrendered himself without condition to Christ as his peace with God. He has awakened to life under the voice of forgiving grace, and his heart glows with the assurance that all is now right between himself and his Sovereign. The morning sun of his soul's Sabbath has risen on his darkness, and is ascending to the meridian of perfect day.

It is none too soon; he was haggard and worn in the long war. His soul was like the bird sent out by Noah. All the world of sin was a shoreless watery waste. With no nourishment and no resting rock, her weary wings were about to fail. It is time the ark was entered. It is time to listen to the Messenger of the covenant's voice to tired wanderers from Jesus, that in him there is rest.

But the change! the change! God, who was dreaded, is now loved. The Majesty which inspired terror is now beheld with open face. The load of unforgiven sin is gone, and the lustings after sin are transformed to aspirations for holiness. The voice so lately feared is music to the soul. The law which condemned is reconciled in Christ. The Divine government, so terrible while its power was arrayed against sin, is now a shield of defence accepted with joy. The everlasting covenant has become the pledge of safety. The renewed man is made to feel himself committed to Christ, under the Father's covenant promise, as the fruit of his sufferings on the cross. Belonging to the Redeemer, as a portion of the promised reward for the offering of his soul for sin, he is not only to shine henceforth in the glory of the mediatorial throne, but to become himself an integral part of that glory. Christ is to be admired in him, and the Spirit is now forming him into such an image as will adorn his Redeemer. For this exalted service he is washed, justified and sanctified. Purchased and wrought for such use, Christ already possesses too precious an interest in him to allow the work to stop incomplete. His Mediator assumes the care of settling his relations with heaven. The Advocate makes all right between the returning sinner and his God. The reconciliation is complete.

Oh, the change! the change! A new world of gladness is opened. The atmosphere which he breathes is joy; peace in believing is his repose. Ashes are exchanged for beauty; mourning for the oil of joy; heaviness for the garment of praise. He lives a new life, and "all that life is love." The deathly darkness of the night of sin has fled before the morning of grace. No lengthening shadows are to mark the decline of this opening day. Its morning is for earth; its meridian, the "sacred, high, eternal noon" of heaven.

"I heard the voice of Jesus say,
  I am this dark world's light;
Look unto me; thy morn shall rise,
  And all thy day be bright.
I looked to Jesus, and I found
  In him my star, my sun,
And in that Light of Life I'll walk
  Till all my journey's done."

## III.

### CONSCIENCE.

#### FIRST—AT WAR.

IN all the moral experiences which have been mentioned, *Conscience* makes itself felt as a power for disquiet or tranquillity. The reproaching conscience agonizes—the approving conscience gives peace.

The power of conscience as an enemy militant, was well illustrated by an occurrence said to have taken place many years ago in one of the western shires of England. A miserable man had crowned a career of wickedness by the commission of a crime of the highest grade of atrocity. He was brought before the assizes on trial for his life. The evidence against him was dark, the countenances of the jurors were portentous and the court was unusually solemn. All appearances conspired to fill him with the worst apprehensions. But, unexpectedly to himself, the skill of his counsel was successful. The course of justice was perverted, and he received a verdict of acquittal. He was once more a free man.

Free—from what? From the court, the bailiff, the iron-bound cell and the executioner; but not from the officer of God. He knew the unsettled wrong between himself and justice. He had the conscience of crime, but not of expiation. He uttered no shout of liberty, but went silently home, threw himself upon his bed, turned upon his face and groaned aloud. A neighbor who came in sought to quiet his distress by repeatedly reminding him that he was *cleared.* The wretched man at length turned himself, and with a stern, desperate look inquired,

"*Where will I find a court to clear me from my own conscience?*" The pangs of his spirit increased from day to day. In less than two weeks he died from no perceptible cause but remorse. Conscience killed him.

O Conscience, what a witness art thou for God in the human breast! Everything else about the mind may be distorted; everything holy lost; the bosom where love should be enthroned given over to the reign of hatred; the passions, which ought to lie still, all in surging strife; the judgment subverted by the malign will, and the reason made irrational on every moral subject; still, amid the perverted and sin-ruined faculties, it holds its integrity as the scorching foe of wrong. It is among the depraved qualities of the mind like Milton's seraph Abdiel in the council of Satan:

"Faithful found
Among the faithless—faithful only he;

Among innumerable false, unmoved,
Unshaken, unseduced, unterrified,
His loyalty he kept."

It is not meant that the faculty of conscience suffered none of the effects of the apostasy in Paradise. Our moral ruin was there complete. There is no attribute in the unrenewed man to which *holiness* can be ascribed. Conscience is deeply implicated in the sad results of sin. The influence of depravity over it is felt in its often becoming remiss, stupefied, or, in the language of Scripture, "seared with a hot iron," so that sinners frequently live for a season unterrified by its reproaches. But the thing meant is, that sooner or later it is sure to awake, and that, when aroused, it takes the part of Heaven against a sinner. As a natural faculty, it takes the side of God whenever it acts at all.

Neither is it meant that it is a teacher of the will of God in general. Gross delusions and wild licentiousness have come from assigning to it a power which it never possessed. It has one great work to do, and in that work it is mighty indeed. It is not its office to teach any moral philosophy or inspired truth beyond this simple proposition—that *right ought always to be practiced, and wrong ought always to be avoided.* No fair construction of Romans ii. 15 will represent it as doing anything more than to *rebuke* or *accuse of wrong* the people mentioned for sinning against those teachings of nature and reason which had just been recited; and nowhere else in the word of God is any other teaching-power ascribed to it. When we would learn what *is* right or wrong, God sends us to his revealed word and to the coincident instructions of our reason. Conscience is given to accuse or excuse; to *enforce* the sense of wrong or justification; to fill the sinner with remorse for known guilt, and to cause the good man to feel the approval of God and become serene.*

The sinner's great war is against God. He has entered the lists with Omnipotence, and this alone will ensure his defeat and the utter prostration of his energies soon. But his strife with conscience takes another direction, which makes the war doubly disheartening. This conscience is a part of his own nature, so that in contending with it he is fighting himself. Here he becomes his own foe. If he triumphs—and he sometimes does for a time, so far as to still the self-accusing voice—he only vanquishes himself; and when he comes to be crushed by remorse, he crushes himself. This is the strange extremity to which he is reduced. In relation to the Divine law, God's views of sin, his dealings with

* The views offered in this paragraph are purposely short of a proper metaphysical discussion, which is not called for in these pages. Just so much is said as will advance the religious purposes of the work.

those who are guilty of it, and his administration in general, the unholy heart is against the Almighty, but the conscience is for him. It is a striking disadvantage on the sinner's side of the contest that he must contend with Heaven and himself at the same time. On the highest throne, one enemy sits; in his own bosom, the other dwells.

If he will persist in such a contest, it can have but one issue. He has made foes to himself, which cannot and should not give him peace or rest. When he approaches the dark valley, deserted by every moral support, remorseful memories wring his heart. He has drawn upon his dying hour the frown of both God above and his conscience within. He is forsaken by heaven and despised by himself.

Every appalling view of his case is aggravated when our thoughts pursue him to the world of spirits. There memory reviews the past—the mercy once offered from the cross, the resistance to that mercy, the calls of the ministry of reconciliation unheeded, the strivings of the Holy Spirit resisted, Sabbaths spent in sin, the work of life neglected through the morning, noon and evening hours of the day of grace, until its sun of hope went down in the night of despair. Then conscience will be felt as the power which arms those recollections with the sting of remorse. Worse than all besides will be the anguish of that long, loud wail, rising distinct from among the moans of the realms of mourning—"*God was right, and I was wrong!*"

Thoughtless reader, does your heart pant to pursue the contest with such a foe? "Lay thine hand upon him; remember the battle; do no more."

# IV.

## CONSCIENCE.

### SECOND—AT PEACE.

A DYING saint had just listened to the reading of the fourteenth chapter of St. John's Gospel. "My son," said he to the reader, "now bring to me the catechism of our Church." The young man brought the book.

"Now read the *Benefits.*" The young man read: "The benefits which in this life do accompany or flow from justification, adoption and sanctification are assurance of God's love, peace of conscience—"

"Stop!" said the dying man, "stop there! let me think of that. Yes, that is it—peace of conscience! Oh, what an enemy conscience once was! What a friend now! How gladly I would have destroyed it then, but what could I now do without its approval? *Peace of conscience*—that is it! Peace through our Lord Jesus Christ! *Peace!* PEACE!"

And yet, viewed as a faculty, this was the same conscience which pursued, even to a despairing death, the guilty wretch spoken of in the commencement of the last chapter. The only difference is that, in this case, it approved and sustained; in the other it stung and crushed. In each alike it was the same faithful witness for God. Its operations vary with the ever-varying states of our souls. The presence or absence of regenerating grace greatly affects its tones, vigilance and power; but through all its different degrees of animation and variety of operations, whenever it does lift its voice, it speaks out for God. The same conscience which affrights the sinner cheers the penitent at the cross and blesses the path of his pilgrimage with peace. The same conscience which creates those frightful spectres which haunt the dying chamber of the unforgiven man, assures the departing saint that all between God and his soul is pleasant. The same conscience which makes the undying worm of future hopeless remorse, dwells delightfully in the bosom of the ransomed saint in glory.

The friend of God feels that his conscience and himself are at peace. It is not meant that his peace springs from a consciousness of personal innocence. He is but a redeemed sinner, whose conscience is purged from dead works by "the blood of Christ, who, through the eternal Spirit, offered *himself without spot* to God." The difference between himself and the sinner out of Christ does not consist in their respective amounts of personal guilt. Out of Christ, both are loaded with sin.

But the one has found refuge from the frown of God under the protection of the cross. His conscience is at peace because the Holy Spirit lays to his soul the assurance that, "if any man sin, we have an advocate with the Father, Jesus Christ the righteous." The other seeks relief from the pangs of an accusing conscience by hardening himself against the reproof and forcing his attention away from his guilt. The whole story was told from the lips of the Christian on the brink of the river, just as we have it from the word of the Holy Spirit—"peace with God through our Lord Jesus Christ." The penitent, thus exalted above the fear which has torment, is no longer afraid to contemplate the past and the present—what he was and what he is. He makes no effort to stupefy his memory of sins, for the recollection of them inspires fresh love of his suffering Lord, upon whom they were laid. The remembrance of his guilt brings him nearer to the cross, and there he hears the voice of forgiveness and feels the conforming power of the Holy Spirit. This Divine work in his soul is what brings himself and his conscience into peace.

It is true there is a spurious trust, which allows of sin that grace may abound. It virtually says, The more sin the better, because the all-forgiving grace of God is then magnified. But *tenderness*, or a quick sensibility to wrong, is one of the special attributes of a good conscience. It revolts from all wrong, feels the shock of sin and rejoices in goodness. As a stimulant to carefulness of life, to an anxious watch against unholiness, and to a prayerful diligence to do the whole will of God, it stands side by side with the Christian graces of faith and love, the best of all guards against the world, the flesh and the devil. The emphatic testimony of the Holy Spirit, already quoted, is that the blood of Christ purges the conscience of the believer from dead works *to serve the living God.* Lifting from the soul the burden of guilt, the peaceful conscience affords its possessor a holy confidence to seek God in prayer, so that he comes boldly to the throne of grace. There, under the Divine brightness, he beholds the beauty of holiness, and longs to have it impressed upon his own heart and exhibited in his whole life. There the condemnation is removed, and the heart thus disburdened is most earnest in its obedience, because its works of well-doing are unterrified and cordial. There is felt that peculiar security for holy living of which the beloved disciple wrote: "Beloved, if our heart condemn us not, then have we confidence toward God. And whatsoever we ask, we receive of him, because we keep his commandments, and do those things that are pleasing in his sight. . . . And he that keepeth his commandments dwelleth in him, and he in him. And hereby we know that he abideth in us, by the Spirit which he hath given us."

PEACE—what beauty dwells in the very word! Still it is not expressive of the feelings now under contemplation without a new and enlarged meaning. Such a meaning it has received in the testamentary promise of Jesus: "Peace I leave with you; my peace I give unto you; *not as the world giveth*, give I unto you."

The mere absence of conflict makes the peace of the world. Carnal views of its blessedness seldom rise above the idea of freedom from disturbing agencies. Exemption from sorrows, fears and contests is all that is essential to the existence of such peace. But if this were all that is implied in the serenity of the conscience which Christ has pacified, what a void there would be in Christian happiness! Every positive element would be removed from celestial peace; the believer's joy would be despoiled of its living essentials, and heavenliness would depart from heaven. Everlasting thanks to Him who, in the school of happy experience, teaches us those sublimer views of peace which behold it as a sanctified quiet under the wing of an approving conscience! We find it not so much in what it removes as in what it imparts.

"*My* peace I give unto you." The blessedness which springs up ever fresh in the Saviour's own heart he shares with his disciple. Once he laid his own soul under the horror of God's frown, and through that he learned, as a thing of personal experience, the joy of deliverance from Divine wrath. Throughout his previous conflicts with the living trials of human life he had derived support and comfort from his Father's smile and his own self-approving conscience. Struggling with the toils of his earthly pilgrimage, bearing up against persecutions and the afflictions which oppressed his mortal nature, the peace which dwelt in his bosom filled him with consolation. The same heavenly inmate diffused its influence over his seasons of communion with the Father, such as we have an example of in the seventeenth chapter of St. John's Gospel. The freedom of intercourse with heaven which he imparts is the same in which his own Spirit delighted. "As thou, Father, art in me, and I in thee, that they also may be one in us." In the placid happiness with which we are filled while enjoying this nearness to the King of heaven we participate in Christ's own bliss. We drink with him at the same fountain of joy and sit in the same bower of delights.

Thus the serenity which we obtain through our Lord Jesus Christ becomes more than a gift *from* the Father of lights. It is literally "the peace *of* God, which passeth all understanding."

# V.

## THE VICTORY THAT OVERCOMETH THE WORLD.

### FIRST—THE RELIANCE.

EACH inwrought spiritual gift has some service for the spiritual man which is peculiarly its own. Faith is the grace for support, for assurance and for victory. The leader of the Israelitish exodus was an example of its *sustaining* power. It is expressly ascribed to his faith, that, through all those long years of discouragement, which would have put any mortal energy out of heart and hope, "he endured as seeing Him who is invisible." When Paul spoke his *assurance* of a house not made with hands, eternal in the heavens, he gave as the ground of it the inworking of God through which he walked by faith, not by sight. But in no respect does faith become to the Christian a higher endowment than when it is felt as a *triumphing* grace. "This is the victory that overcometh the world, even our faith." First bringing the believer into union with Christ, it works through all its other influences up to that highest triumph where he can say that in tribulation, distress, persecution, famine, nakedness, peril or sword—in death, life, things present or to come—in all these things he is more than conqueror through Him that loved him.

We reach heaven only through victory. The triumphs of the redeemed soul, present or final, are a victor's triumphs. The crowns which are worn by glorified saints are victors' crowns; the palms which they bear are victors' palms. "They *overcame* by the blood of the Lamb" Where there is conquest, there has been conflict. Victory is the turning-point in the fortunes of war. It is the end of strife. It is accounted great and glorious only when the strife has been fierce and deadly.

Where there is strife there is a foe. The believer is in life-and-death conflict with principalities and powers—the rulers of the darkness of this world; and it is *through* as well as *in* this world they rule. He breasts the great army of worldly influences, arrayed to cut off his march toward heaven and crowd him down to ruin. We are told of the world, the flesh and the devil, as the three great enemies standing in array between the soul and heaven. But as the flesh is only a species of the genus world, and as through worldly seductions the devil gains the mastery, the victory that overcomes the world becomes a victory over all, or the failure to overcome the world is a failure of all. If, as the issue of the conflict, an immortal soul is lost and sinks to the everlasting ruin, it is because the world is victor in the fight. If, on the other hand, that soul escapes the ruin, and from the dying bed soars away to the immortal life, it is the victory that overcometh the world.

For this victory the enlisted Christian soldier strikes out. But let him mark well the whole ground of his hopes of triumph—the force for reliance, the plan of the campaign and the discipline of the field. In common war the laying out of campaigns upon impracticable theories, the working of weapons which can do no execution, or the occupation of lines from which there is no possible road to victory, are worse than a waste of strength. It brings in the end a defeat more productive of suffering than would have followed an early surrender. In the soul's warfare for the heavenly victory an analogous folly would result only from a neglect to study the force and means at command. God has mapped out for those who will adopt it a campaign which is incapable of failure; he has arranged for those who will make it their position, a line from which no storm of battle can drive them; and he supplies the force in which from that line they can bear down upon flying foes, open the way to the land of conquest, and from thence send back the shout of finished victory.

Then what is this victory that overcometh the world?

Faith, passing up through lesser meanings, is complete only in this—a perfect *reliance* on the sufficiency of Christ; the *leaning* of the believer on the atonement and intercession of the Redeemer *for* him and his grace *in* him. Mental belief in the doctrine of the cross, obedient belief and unquestioning belief, are all involved in this. Sweet and submissive confidence in the promises is also included—such as the promise of present support and coming deliverance under all trials of flesh or spirit where patience in suffering is called for. In Hebrews xi. we have the finest illustrations on record of the manifestations of faith in obedient and unquestioning submission to the will of God, both in doing and suffering. The definition given to it in the first verse of the chapter speaks a volume of power to work the Christian life into its highest activities: "Faith is the substance of things hoped for; the evidence of things not seen." Here is a higher principle of either activity or endurance than mere *hope.* The word *earnest* comes nearer to it—a word implying foretaste as well as expectation—a specimen of the promised good now in hand, as well as an assurance of the whole to come. But beyond even this there lies, in the terms quoted, the idea of a true forestalling of the possession, making a present now of the glorious hereafter—in fact, making the coming glory so powerfully present to the feelings that the really present toils and sufferings are felt as things of the past. This, we are then told, was the power which wrought those wondrous acts of obedience, patience and endurance in Noah, Abraham, Moses and other ancient worthies, who, because they believed God, came off victors in the battle with the world. They endured as seeing Him who is invisible; they had respect unto the recompense of the reward.

But even this view of faith, as the substance of the things hoped for and the evidence of things not seen, fails to account for those high moral achievements, except as it is regarded in its relation to the cross. We must go back to the underlying import of the term before stated, which lends reality and vitalizing energy to its lesser meanings—reliance on Christ. It puts on this fullness of meaning in the first experience of every true Christian.

The first motion of the regenerate heart is one of reliance on the sufficiency of Christ as the Saviour of the soul. It is a plain, intelligible feeling—one that can be put into language as well as felt in the heart. Parting from all vain notions of self-justification, the believer accepts the justifying grace of the atonement as a provision for himself. He does not believe the story of the death of Jesus merely as he believes the history of the wars of Julius Cæsar. His heart is not affected by the wrong done to the victim of the cross in the way that it is softened by the dying scene of Socrates. Neither does his interest in the atonement rest at the conclusion that there is fullness in it for the redemption of *some* sinners. But, coming with his own broken heart to the cross, and feeling himself one of the sinners for whom such expiation was needed, and one of those for whom it was really made, his believing and appropriating faith looks up to the cross and says—

"There hung the man that died for *me*."

Here is the conquest of self, the first

triumph of faith and the grasping of the true force for all succeeding triumphs.

We expect no victory for the soldier who goes into the field of strife in worthless armor, against overwhelming odds, and relying upon imaginary reinforcements never to appear. Such is all the sinner's hope of overcoming the world without Christ in him and for him. Influences hostile to grace have control of his heart. There is treason within, and through that he is disarmed of all strength for the conflict with evil. His moral powers feel the inspiration of no living hatred of sin; no revolt from the slavery of worldly influences excites his efforts to break the chain. If he feels the strife at all, every pleading of his own nature is for the enemy. Even stronger against him than the world without are the corrupt forces which his own bosom nourishes. The experience of millions corroborates the Divine testimony, that before he can hope for victory over the world the conquest of himself must be made. The forces within him must be so thoroughly revolutionized in spirit that they will take the side of his soul against Satan.

But how is this first battle to be fought? And who shall achieve this first victory—the victory within and over himself? The answer is short, satisfactory and scriptural. The battle *has been* fought, and the victory is to-day laid at the sinner's feet, awaiting only reception by his faith to become *his* victory. It is an old point—one of the elementary principles of the great atonement. We were helpless in the strife against our own corrupt propensities. We had no power left to free ourselves from the bondage, and no price to purchase a ransom from it. There Christ met us. In the blood of his cross he paid the ransom. Alone he fought all the power arrayed for our eternal slavery to sin, and in his conquest over hell he broke that power for all who, with appropriating faith, looking up to him as a personal Redeemer, can say, "My Lord and my God!" Coming to him for the victory which he on Calvary wrought for his people; approaching with hearts longing to find in it triumph over sin as well as deliverance from wrath; yielding our entire confidence to the reality and sufficiency of this work of Christ; appropriating to ourselves the Lord Jesus as our righteousness,—this is the faith which makes the victory of Christ to become in ourselves our victory. It is the beginning of the victory that overcometh the world.

# VI.

## THE VICTORY THAT OVERCOMETH THE WORLD.

### SECOND—ENDURANCE.

WITH Christ living in the heart by a relying faith, "greater is he that is in you than he that is in the world." Thus we become armed for the conflict to come. Conflict *to come?* After what has been said of Christ having alone fought the battle for us against the powers of darkness, and of his having achieved the victory and given it over to us as our victory, is there still conflict to come? Yes, enough of watching against spiritual foes, of wrestlings with fightings without and fears within, and of strife with worldly influences in every form in which they can be arrayed against the soul, to make felt the value of faith as an armor in that part of the conflict which is now laid upon ourselves. The faith through which the victory of the cross first became our victory must abide to the end; and upheld by it, while we wrestle and pray and endure, all must be the working of the power of the atonement in us. We are saved only as we ourselves endure to the end; but when that end comes, we can only say as one dying Christian said, "*I* have not run—*Christ* carried me; *I* have not worked—*Christ* wrought in me; *I* have not conquered—*Christ* vanquished for me: *Christ* has done all."

It is an important point, and vital to a well-maintained Christian experience, that, while in the redemption of the believer from the bondage of corruption, Christ, without him, and alone upon Calvary, achieved the victory, in the conflict with opposing powers which he is to carry on to the end, Christ only works with him and through him. In the war with the world and sin "*we* must fight if we would reign." We must win the crowns we would wear; we must suffer with Jesus if we would be glorified with him. Our Christian course in this world begins with our Lord's victory; our own lies at the end. The crown of our redemption already adorns the Redeemer's brow; our own is laid up, not to be bestowed upon any one until he can say, "I have fought the good fight"—not I *am fighting* it, but I *have fought* it—"I have finished my course; I have kept the faith."

In this life-long conflict of our own we find the full value of that highest character of Christian faith which makes it a reliance upon the all-sufficiency of Christ. Here it becomes to us incitement, support, endurance and the substance of the victory to come. The greatness and glory of its achievements reveal the sublime greatness of the grace itself. We see it in the examples already referred to, recorded in Hebrews xi.—examples which are not to be thrown out as irrelevant to *Christian* faith because they were anterior to the great Christian sacrifice, for all the power of grace in our world before the actual occurrence of Christ's earthly mission was substantially the power of the cross. True, it was darkly, and only in expectation such; but from the hour of the promise that the seed of the woman should bruise the serpent's head, the power of Christ resting in his people has been the only effective antagonism to sin—the only support of the patience of the saints. And so, astonished at the magnitude of the grace which can thus appropriate this power, we read how faith girded men of God to subdue kingdoms, work righteousness, obtain promises, stop the mouths of lions, quench the violence of fire, escape the edge of the sword and to turn to flight the, armies of the aliens. We read how they were sustained by its strength, while, not accepting deliverance, they were stoned, were sawn asunder, were tempted, were slain with the sword, or while, driven from society and from employment because of their fidelity to God, they wandered about in sheepskins and goatskins, being destitute, afflicted, tormented—wandered in deserts and mountains and dens and caves of the earth.

These are not to be passed off as the characteristics of the earlier times of the Church, or a type of consecration which belonged only to the martyr ages. It is, in more or less measure, the one faith of all the children of our King; and such it will remain until all who wear it as their armor in the conflict have passed over to the land of the conquerors. No generation passes without furnishing illustrious examples of its power for support and comfort, for faithful action on the field, and for calm endurance and assured hope in the floods.

We see one making an open profession of the name of Christ. We know his history, his social relations and his constitutional temperament, and we know the conflict of spirit which must grow out of them. We see him rising above the natural timidity of his shrinking nature, and above the social influences which are in active array against his resolved consecration to Jesus. We see him walk with unblenching brow abreast of obloquy and reproach—in fact abreast of every feeling within, and every influence without, to which his nature was once accustomed to yield. His resolution conquers all; he forsakes all to follow Christ. What does it mean? It is the victory that overcometh the world, even his faith. We next watch the progression of his Christian life. All the influences around him—social, financial, political, or any way affecting what are seemingly his worldly interest—suggest a lax piety, and invite to compromises with the world. They seem to lie in the direction of the friendship of the world, which is enmity with God. They frown upon a religion of open and earnest fidelity to Christ and his truth, and propose in its place a retiring and non-aggressive piety. But we see him, out of his warm heart for Jesus, breaking through every snare spread across his pilgrim path, and in all duty, in the sight of men, taking up his cross of doing and enduring for Christ. We see in him the spirit of constant communion with God, the daily crucifixion of inbred lusts, the living down of corrupt desires and unholy affections, and growing heavenly-mindedness and ripeness for heaven. Again we inquire how all this comes: we meet the same answer—it is the victory of faith over the world.

We see another. He is a young man

—the son in a home where there is purity, refinement and wealth. He is bound to that home by the tenderest love. But he turns thoughtfully and resolutely away from its endearments, because from the far-off homes of sin he has heard the cry, "Come over and help us!" We read his reply to the Missionary Board, who have inquired what his wishes concerning a location are: "When I gave myself to Christ, I did it *unconditionally.* In like manner I give myself to this work. As regards my place of labor, I have no wish but to obey the call of God. If in the great world, which must all be brought in for Christ, there are places of peculiar unpleasantness and exposure, I would not presumptuously seek them, but if the providence of God point the way thither, I would say, 'Speak, Lord; thy servant heareth.' Christ has done more for me than I can ever do for him. My prayer is, that I may, more and more, make it my meat and drink to do his will."

There is still another—a toiler in a humbler field, but useful in inverse ratio to its lowliness. We see her in the byways of our cities, or among the wilds of our country, with Bibles and tracts in her hand and prayer in her heart, going from house to house, inquiring for the welfare of souls, bowing meekly under abuse, bearing with the hardened, instructing the anxious, and cheering the neglected with thoughts of Christ here and heaven in sight. She has voluntarily chosen a path which leads away from public honors. Hers is an unobserved work. But where she walks the footsteps of the Holy Spirit are seen. In many dark corners of the land, she has been, and when she had gone people thought of her visits, and then thought of better things, for they felt that God had been with them.

Subsequent articles will exhibit the

power of this victory which overcomes the word, amid other fields of the Christian conflict, especially in sorrow, suffering and death; and in all it will be found, as the hiding of its power, that it bears the character already ascribed to it—a reliance on the all-sufficiency of Christ. In every phase and every turning period in this conflict, in all those strifes within the heart known only to itself and God, in bearing the cross of the holy activities of religion, and in receiving the whole baptism of sorrow which the heavenly Father appoints, the truth is made good, that "this is the victory that overcometh the world, even our faith." From the hour of spiritual conversion to that of the final departure for glory, it is a faithful and joyous truth—how joyous, can never be told in the language of earth.

# VII.

## ASSURANCE.

### FIRST—A LAWFUL EXPECTATION.

THE fountain of joy which the Saviour has opened for his friends is full and overflowing. Why, then, should they stint themselves when they come to it for supplies? Why not believe the full value of the boon, and honor the benefactor by accepting his generosity precisely as it is offered? The believer remembers how it was with him on the deserts of sin, with no cooling spring at hand. He remembers the thirst which nothing in those arid regions could assuage. He knew—for it was a *felt* experience—that his soul must drink or die; and what had all this world of sin to offer for the relief of such anguish? That which, in the distance, seemed a refreshing water, was found, on a near approach, to be a deceitful mirage; and what could he do?

A fountain was opened for sin and uncleanness. The voice of eternal Mercy cried, "*Ho, to the waters!*" He listened; he approached, knelt and bathed his parched lips in the river of salvation. Fresh from such an experience of the pangs of sin, it ill behooves him to disdain the relief from all its terrors which is offered in the *full assurance* that his sins are forgiven, and that, through the grace which completes what it begins, he, enduring to the end, shall be saved.

This ground is generally approached with the most solemn caution by the truest Christians. So it should be. Fools only would "rush in" here. Concerning the matter of personal salvation, the loftiest hope to which some dare aspire consists in a sweet reconciliation to all the judgments of God, and a willingness to leave their souls at his disposal. With the king of Israel they say, "Let us fall now into the hands of the Lord, for his mercies are great." The language of such submission is substantially this: I am a guilty sinner, hopeless except from the mercy of God in Christ Jesus. Without Christ for my Advocate and Saviour from wrath, I cannot stand a moment in judgment with God. Out of him, I am a doomed victim of eternal justice. All that I can do is to renounce sin with loathing, yield myself to Christ as my Mediator with God, and then strive to walk in newness of life. As far as I know my own heart, I give myself to the Saviour upon his own terms, and, God being my helper, I will consecrate my ability for usefulness and myself to him. I can do no more; and in the daily doing of this I am willing to leave all else with

God. The Judge of all the earth will do right. My care shall terminate in the question, What am I to do? and God shall then do what he pleases with me.

This experience reveals an evangelical and pleasant state of mind. It speaks sweet submission to the Divine government, supreme consecration to the work of God, and confidence that the mercy of the atonement will be rightly exercised. Happy are those who can expose such a heart to the scrutiny of the heart-searching Spirit! But the question whether this experience, submissive and trusting as it is, comes up to the proper measure of a Christian hope depends upon the answer to this further inquiry, Is it all the attainment which God now proposes to his friends? When it is reached, is the mission of the Comforter, as described in the New Testament, fulfilled? The soul, escaping from the gloom and sorrow of sin, should seek the choicest repose which the mercy of God provides. While seeking our bliss from the comforts of the Holy Ghost, nothing is enough, while the way is open for the enjoyment of more. Inferior attainments are vantage-grounds, upon which we should stand and gird ourselves to reach unto those things which are before.

We certainly read of "*the full assurance of hope.*"

No attempted exposition has ever been able to give to those words any other than their most natural meaning—an entire confidence of possessing a present and eternal interest in the blessings of the atonement. This assured hope is the offspring of faith. That faith rests in the Promiser as true, and then in the promises as applying specifically to the believer.

A man holds a bank-note. He first inquires respecting the character of the bank, and becomes satisfied that it may be relied on for the redemption of its paper. This resembles that first degree of confidence in God, which regards his provision for saving *all who in true faith receive Christ*, as full and certain to be carried out. In this confidence a man may doubt whether *he is himself a subject of that provision*, but he has no doubt that every promise of God will be fulfilled.

The holder of the bank-note next inquires into the *genuineness* of the particular bill in his hand. If on examination it does not prove a counterfeit, then he feels assured that he holds the promise of the bank *to himself*, and he expects to enjoy the *personal* benefit of that promise, So the Christian's faith in the general promises of redeeming mercy ripens to the full assurance of hope when he enjoys a sufficiency of evidence that these promises *apply specifically to his own case*, as one who comes properly within the provisions of the covenant of redemption. For then the promises of that covenant are *to him personally* a pledge of salvation.*

Far be it from us to regard personal safety from final wrath as the ultimate object of Christian ambition. The sanctified heart looks beyond all the benefits of the cross to the creatures of God, and rejoices with unspeakable joy while it beholds all these lesser results conspiring to bring glory to God, through the service and everlasting bliss of a redeemed people. And that is a precious faith which enables the Christian, while consecrating himself to the whole work laid to his hands, to resolve all desires for himself into acquiescence in the Divine will.

* The illustration from the bank-note is suggested by Dr. Thomas Scott, who, in his Commentary, adopts a present and full assurance of a saving interest in Christ as the meaning of the apostle in Hebrews vi. 11. He regards the "assurrance of *faith*," not "*hope*," mentioned in Hebrews x. 22, as amounting *only* to the confidence of the bill-holder in the *responsibility of the bank*. The question whether this is not too close a limitation of that faith is not pertinent to the present work.

Still, the *casting out of fear* is essential to the highest enjoyment of the hope of heaven. Until we feel our views settled respecting our own standing in Christ, it is hardly possible to conceive of such a submission as leaves no room for the anxious inquiry, What will be the issue of the Divine will in my case? It would seem as if such a question must agitate even the saint in glory, notwithstanding all his confidence in the Divine rectitude, if there were really any uncertainty about his eternal continuance in that world. It is true he might be quietly submissive —perhaps in the main happily submissive—but could he close his bosom against *fear?* Yet fear must be expelled before the soul will find perfect peace in Christ, " because fear hath torment."

When God, for the quickening of our piety, spreads before us the joyous things of religion, he does not refer us to quiet submission alone. He exhibits HOPE as an anchor fastening the soul to moorings within the veil, and he tells of strong consolation for those who have fled to the refuge of this hope. The vessel anchored in the stream is moved by the winds and tides, but whichever way she is blown or drifted, her prow turns always toward the spot to which she is fastened. The tempest which disturbs the waters where she rides never turns her eyes from the place where her anchor is fastened.

So we lie in the stream of time, awaiting the appointed hour to spread our sails for the ocean of eternity. God means that, in the interval, our hope, "as an anchor of the soul, both sure and steadfast, and which entereth into that within the veil," shall keep our attention delightfully engaged on what awaits us there. He has given the "hope of salvation" to be the helmet of the Christian warrior, that in all his conflicts with fear within and fightings without, he may "rejoice in hope of the glory of God," and be refreshed and assured of final victory. It will be sad for him, if he allows the popular prejudice against the "full assurance of hope" to score down this grace to any lesser power for consolation than that with which God has clothed it.

But the question whether assurance is, in the present life, a fairly attainable grace, and therefore a lawful object of expectation, is best answered by referring to what has actually occurred. When a man of God said, "I know that my Redeemer liveth," and then added the explicit expression of his perfect confidence that he should see him with joy in the resurrection, he spoke words to which we can attach but one meaning. He had the "full assurance of hope." The language of another Bible saint is also unequivocal: "I am persuaded that neither death, nor life, nor angels, nor principalities, nor powers, nor things present, nor things to come, nor height, nor depth, nor any other creature, shall be able to separate us from the love of God, which is in Christ Jesus our Lord." The beauty of this assurance again glows from another earnest testimony from the same Christian: "I am now ready to be offered, and the time of my departure is at hand. I have fought a good fight; I have finished my course; I have kept the faith; henceforth there is laid up for me a crown of righteousness, which the Lord, the righteous Judge, shall give me at that day."

These experiences are of unmistakable import, and they are examples of many others recorded with evident approval by the Spirit of inspiration. In relating them, no care is used to guard the language with any such qualifying terms as might warn the reader against making their meaning too positive. The relator does not even suggest that his feelings are peculiar or rare, but he speaks of what he enjoys as we now speak of common graces. So when the Apostle John tells his brethren that, by loving in deed and truth, they shall assure their hearts before God, he passes on without pausing to modify or explain his words. He does not seem to think that he is wandering so far from the common track of Christian experience that what he says will be obscure or surprising. Peter offered no apology for presuming to appeal to the omniscience of his Lord for the certainty of his love. It is evident that, when these things were spoken, the cold warning to beware of expecting too much had not gone abroad. With Christians, the full assurance of hope unto the end appears to have been a mark for attainment too common and too well understood to require explanation.

It is here worthy of notice that the "glimmering" and half-established hope is nowhere in the Bible set up as the mark of Christian lowliness of mind or of the evangelical feeling of ill-desert. The notion which associates them is a man-begotten one, if not worse. It is a notion which fails to take into account the blood of Jesus as prevailing against all the unworthiness of the believer. The Holy Scriptures often enjoin upon Christians to cherish lowly views of themselves, and we read much of this in the experience of New Testament saints; but very rarely do we read of one of them as cherishing any doubt of his acceptance with God. We now hear so much of these doubts, as a thing to be expected in our religious experience, that it would surprise many readers to observe how rarely the Word of God makes any allusion to them. True—and to this we shall soon more distinctly refer—it enjoins earnest self-examination; it warns us earnestly of the perils of presumption, and it reveals the fearful fact that many are expecting heaven who will never reach that world. But the Holy Spirit has never taught us to infer from this awful truth that the hope of assurance is a dangerous object of ambition; neither does our common sense require any such conclusion. In the New Testament we read much of false professors, but we read almost nothing of doubting or gloomy Christians. All its language betrays the expectation that the sons of God will be the children of peace and joy—that they will know their living Redeemer, and, looking upon heaven as their own, will ever pursue their pilgrim march thither under unclouded skies.

The doubt of acceptance obtains all its show of modesty from that forced association with Christian lowliness of mind which has been named. Removed from this arbitrary association, it stands forth as unamiable in itself, as it is unlike the sons of God. If it arises from a discovery of past sin, it betrays imperfect views of the nature and power of redemption. If it results from an unsettled feeling respecting the question whether we have come within the terms of mercy, it exhibits the soul lingering over an inquiry which ought to be answered one way or the other. It holds its victim to a point from which he ought to remove at once. If it arises from any apprehension respecting the security of the eternal covenant of redemption, it is next to infidelity. In any point of view, a cherished doubt wars against the Christian's peace and holiness, and thrusts itself between the believer and his Saviour.

Two things have chilled the ambition of many who should now be living in one joy of assurance. One is the fear of vain glory: the other, the disgust with which they have looked upon some miserable professions of this attainment.

But it should be remembered that the belief of possessing large measures of Divine influence makes only hypocrites proud. Such there always have been, and will be for long years to come. It pleases God to try his own children, by allowing such persons to expose religion to shame; and the endurance of this reproach is a part of the patience of the saints. Great sanctity and positive hopes, with no better evidence than "*Thus I feel*," or, "*Thus I was told in a vision with a great flood of light*," will be professed by men who afford no rational proof of one godly exercise. Such persons will be proud, vain boasters, whose influence will mortify Christians and subject the cause of Christ to disaster.

But when the Redeemer's true friends allow themselves to trifle with valuable privileges because these empty boasts are so loathsome, they give to bad men a power over their own experience which properly belongs to the Holy Spirit alone. They allow sinners to prescribe the measure of their own attainments. There is nothing in grace to make its subject vainglorious. We scandalize the Spirit when we shrink from accepting its highest comforts through fear that they will turn us into silly braggarts. Standing in Christ, where alone undeserving sinners enjoy the hopes of the covenant, deeper humility results from each fresh discovery of God's favor to us. As grace after grace, poured without stint into the soul, brings out the cry, "*What peace! what bliss!*" it just as inevitably awakens the reflection, "*Upon how unworthy an object is it bestowed!*" No others are so sure of God's eternal love as the already glorified spirits: no others, with so profound a disclaiming of personal worthiness, looking up to the enthroned Redeemer,

"Spread their trophies at his feet,
And crown him Lord of all."

# VIII.

## ASSURANCE.

### SECOND—THE WITNESS OF THE SPIRIT.

NO inspired writer's language bears more the appearance of well-considered meaning than that of Paul. There is no reason for divesting the term of its exact sense, when he says to the Corinthian brethren (2d Epist. chap. v.), "We *know* that if our earthly house of this tabernacle were dissolved, we have a building of God, a house not made with hands, eternal in the heavens." No other insight which his epistles afford to his experience will justify us in grading this confidence as a merely comparative one, or anything less than absolute.

And yet our knowledge of him and of ourselves—of him as one of ourselves—forbids the thought that this assurance was the product of his own mind, or was reached through his own ordinary reasoning faculties alone. The power is not in us to come to so certain a conclusion concerning our moral condition. Our self-consciousness, our judgment and our faculties throughout are too finite, too infirm and too often convicted of mistake to render a confidence thus begotten anything less than a daring presumption. To be in any of us what it was in Paul, it must be something of communication to our minds, something *brought in*, something wrought into a certainty by the Infallible Mind, and communicated to ours with the Divine signature. We need no more lucid description of this wonderful revelation than that in Romans viii. 16, written also by Paul: "The Spirit itself beareth witness with our spirit, that we are the children of God."

Turning again to the assurance expressed in the first quotation above, and reading a little farther, we find the support to which this "*we know*" is fastened. "Now he that hath wrought us for the selfsame thing is God, *who also hath given unto us the earnest of the Spirit.* THEREFORE we are always confident." In the *earnest* of a possession there are involved the two elements of some present foretaste and an expectation of the future enjoyment of the whole. Such was the cluster of grapes brought by the spies from Canaan to the anxious multitude in the wilderness. It assured the people that Canaan was no fiction; that there lay the land to which God was leading them; and it gave them a foretaste of its fruits. So while the Comforter gives to the believer's soul the expectation of future glory, it brings down many ante-pasts of the joy which there awaits him—"celestial fruits on earthly ground."

But let us not, because of the communicative origin of the hope of assurance, make it too exclusively miraculous, or release our reasoning powers from all duty concerning it, and straiten it to an operation on the feelings alone. God meant that the testimony of the Spirit should join in with some co-operating power within us for reaching conclusions. The Spirit must bear witness with our spirit—a conference of testimony—and thus the conclusion be made satisfying to us. But if satisfying, it must be something that is explicit. We are not to become mere imbeciles in the act of casting ourselves with unbounded reliance upon hopes for the eternal world; but what less are we if we utterly discard the reflective faculties, and venture all upon the *impressions* of the moment? There are other spirits besides that of God which have power to impress the human feelings. It would be a criminal folly to stake a hope of salvation upon the bare fact that *something* brought the word to our hearts that all is well. In commanding us to "try the spirits, whether they are of God," our heavenly Father has not left us without the means of subjecting the work of his own Spirit to the scrutiny of the common rules of evidence. He allows the operations of the Spirit to be examined in the light of our understanding, at least so far as to enable us, when satisfied that we really enjoy its earnest, "to give an answer to every man that asketh a *reason* of the hope that is in us."

There is here no inconsistency with the higher truth that there are transactions between the Divine Spirit and the soul which can never come under human modes of explanation. The things of Christ are showed to the divinely-illuminated heart with ineffable clearness and by a process which cannot be described. The Spirit's witness for the believer that he is a child of God is *immediate with his own spirit.* The earnest of heaven which it affords consists in the *direct communication* of celestial views to his mind and the feelings of the glorified to his heart.

Yet even this spiritual intercourse is not through vague impressions, which admit of no external proof of their genuineness. The Spirit performs other offices which the understanding *can* estimate; and that part of his work which *is* observable is made an indispensable evidence that we are under his power. He is the author of the word of divine inspiration. In that volume of revelation the Spirit describes the way by which a sinner comes to Christ: Did we come by that new and living way? There he convinces of sin: Have our souls bowed in sorrow under the burden of guilt? He convinces of righteousness and of judgment: In the light of God's holy government have we sought our justification in Christ alone, and have we fled to his atonement for refuge from final wrath? The Spirit exhibits a list of Christian characteristics which afford evidence of his work in the heart: Are these fruits found in our own character and lives? As men, are we honest, unselfish, self-controlling, gentle, and faithful to the calls of humanity? As Christians, are we prayerful, humble, crucified to the world, free to meet the calls upon our Christian benevolence, self-denying in our Saviour's service, in sympathy with the institutions of the Church, in love with the brethren and walking with God? Is this frame of mind habitual, and is it developed in our common intercourse with the world?

The list of *rational* evidences might be extended much farther. They are tests which the Spirit itself has furnished in its own book of truth and duty. It bears its testimony for them, that they are true, gracious traits. By spreading before us so many comprehensible points for self-examination, it affords such witness of piety in the soul as the common judgment can approve. When *through the truth* it has borne such testimony toward sustaining a hope of heaven, the way is prepared to accept without distrust the higher witness which it bears *with the heart.* The internal impression is then known as true, because the Spirit has been tried, and has been found to speak as God speaks in his revealed word. The union of the Spirit's outward rational evidence and its inwrought witness with the believer's spirit removes the last vestige of condemning fear, and his confidence becomes implicit and imperishable.

An assurance gained and preserved only upon such conditions can never admit of carelessness respecting self-examination. It is a mistake to suppose that self-examination necessarily implies the existence of doubt. There is no evidence, either from the Scriptures in connection or from any other source, that Paul's confidence had faltered, when he spoke of bringing his body into subjection, " lest by any means, when I have preached to others, I myself should be a castaway." There is no absurdity in imagining an angel often looking over the tenure by which he holds his place in Paradise, and deriving pleasure from reviewing the ground on which he stands. So the assured Christian will consider the experience of his heart, and the whole working of the justifying and sanctifying grace within him, to be refreshed by the Spirit's approbation of it all. The contemplation of hopes thus sustained involves the review of all the evidences which sustain them. The assurance of hope, viewed in this light, secures a constant heart-watch, and there is no danger that its enjoyment will render self-examination a farce. The same view removes the apprehension that it will promote carelessness respecting active duty. It is maintained *in* duty, and the Spirit lifts up its accusing voice against every sinful neglect. More than this, joy and love are stronger incentives to well-doing than fear. The more these are shed abroad in the soul, so much the more the Christian will watch and pray, and so much the better he will live.

Through such earnest and witness the believer learns to recognize the whispers of the Spirit in his soul, "Be of good cheer; thy sins be forgiven thee;" "I have called thee by name; thou art mine." Persuaded that this unclouded expectation of heaven is a real and attainable grace, and that, when possessed, it imparts more celestial joy than is ever experienced in its absence, we again ask ourselves why we should .abridge the privilege which the covenant of grace opens? Whatever heavenly good our Lord sets before us, he wishes us to enjoy and expects us to seek. He knows best what comforts are most appropriate for us this side of the veil, and all the repose to which he invites us is safe.

It is a poor satisfaction to be told that assurance *may be* an attainable grace, but it is not to be expected in one case out of a thousand. We have too long measured our expectations by the spiritual experience current since the departure of the intense consecration of primitive Christianity. We look back to the times of Jesus on earth and of his apostles, and we find it assumed in all their instructions that this strong consolation was to be a prevalent solace in the Church. Neither do we find comfort in being told that the Christian *may* reach this assurance before he dies, but if so it is probably in store for a few of his last moments on earth—the dying grace for a dying hour. Such speculations do more than chill us; they seem to trifle with the fixed arrangements and conditions of our existence. They make a third state of being between the present and the eternal, as if the last moments of life were not subject to the same reason and laws of evidence with those which preceded them. It is true that God has peculiar consolations for seasons of peculiar need; and this fact is often vividly realized in the hour when heart and flesh are failing. But nowhere this side of heaven are we to expect a revelation of new principles of judgment or new evidences of piety, beyond those which are now within our reach.

Then be it ours to find our highest rest of soul where others have found it—rest from all feeling of condemnation now, and all apprehension of it to come, because we know that *our* Redeemer liveth, and we expect to be satisfied when we awake with his likeness.

# IX.

## LOVE.

### FIRST—THE CHIEF GRACE.

SHOULD we look no farther than its power for joy unspeakable we should still unhesitatingly adopt the apostle's grading, which ranks love as the highest in the triad of graces. What a new world of holy tranquillity is revealed in the experience which proves that "there is no fear in love, but perfect love casteth out fear, because fear hath torment!"

The influence of *conscience* in affording serenity or anguish has been mentioned; but that does not bring us up to the mark of the power of our affections for joy or sorrow. Peace of conscience is indeed a delightful attainment: joy to the reconciled offender who can lay his hand on his breast and say, It is mine! But we must rise higher than that. For the pain or pleasure which flows to us through the working of the natural conscience is not inherent in the faculty itself. Conscience is simply an index pointing us to something outside of itself, as the occasion of the distress or comfort which it gives. It produces remorse or peace, not by drawing upon its own nature, but by assuring us that God is angry or complacent. But the *affections* are, in themselves, full of joy or grief—a well-spring of comfort or a boiling sea of torment. Love, if it be right and happily requited, imparts bliss from its own nature. On the other hand, it is in the very nature of improper affections to produce misery in the heart which cherishes them.

Selfishness affords a striking example of this. It closes the heart against the noble sentiment of universal brotherhood and excites bitter envy in view of the happiness of others. By arraigning the interest of its subject against that of the rest of mankind, it keeps him on the rack of apprehension, where he trembles to trust any of his kind. Love, that richest treasure of the heart, is exhausted in self-interest; and the inevitable consequence of this misapplying of affection is seen in coldness of heart and sourness of temper, sometimes concealed under a false affability, but often acted out in undisguised moroseness. Here is displeasure in the happiness of others, a nervous dread of mankind, a locking of the soul against human sympathy and an asperity of spirit, expressed by unamiable conduct or concealed under the fretting mask of hypocrisy. If these do not constitute a life of pain, then rest may be enjoyed on a bed of thorns.

But it is not alone in the bad affections that the power of love for sorrow as well as joy is illustrated. Those human fondnesses which are lawful, and, in themselves, even virtuous and adapted to the purest earthly joy, often become the very steepings of the cup of anguish; and this fact suggests one of the most vivid views of the superior excellence of that love of God which the Spirit sheds abroad in the sanctified heart—the *perfect love* which casts out fear and has no torment. Look at one who has expended all the fondness of a true and trusting heart upon some object which at last betrays the adoring love which it has secured, and requites a long and earnest attachment with unfeeling scorn. The first knowledge of this perfidy falls like a thunderbolt on the heart, and it is often followed by consuming grief which longs to hide itself in the grave.

And even where love is well placed and well requited we have seen mournful exemplications of the same truth, that the purest and happiest earthly affections often become the source of unspeakable sorrow. The dearest human delights which the fall has left to our race are gathered around the altars of home. They live in the smiles, the tenderness and the thousand nameless endearments of the hearthstone. There the heart of care loves to unburden itself and be at peace. Thither stern manhood retires from the irritating conflicts of life, and, for a little while, exchanges the conflicts without for the love within. There the child buries his face in his mother's bosom, weeps his little grief away and looks up all radiant with happiness. There is the highest illustration which the world affords of the power of the natural affections for producing human bliss.

And there, beyond all other places else, exists the mournful proof that their strength for sorrow is exactly commensurate with their strength for joy. The mother, watching the expiring life of her infant; the child, standing by the dying bed of his last earthly parent, and, when all is over, shying away to a corner and, under the first overwhelming shock of orphanage, sobbing as if his little heart would break; the wife—a wife no more—standing by the grave where they are putting into darkness him for whose sake she loved to live and be happy: these can tell us too truly that the depth of their love makes the depth of their grief. Had they loved less they would sorrow less.

Discovering in our own moral natures the necessity for both the inflow and outflow of fond affection, and witnessing so much sorrow in the train of human attachments, how refreshing is the revelation of a love which is ever joyous and satisfying, because it is planted, nurtured, shed abroad, by the Holy Spirit in the heart! We yield to this influence without fear of ill-requital, without dread of losing the objects of our delight, and without any apprehension that we are preparing the way for trials by allowing our affections to become too intense. The bliss which it affords our spirits is in proportion to the fullness of its in-dwelling. When it becomes perfect it will cast out all fear. To the serenity of the pacified conscience we give the name of *peace*. The pleasure which divine love inspires is better expressed by the term *bliss*. Wielding all the power for happiness which the affection of human love possesses, and then, by linking itself to the Divine nature, ethe-realizing both itself and its fruits, it is no longer an earthly, but a heavenly princi-ple; no more a human, but an immortal sentiment, ripening the soul for the ec-stasy of heaven.

In its manifestations it has variety, but in its substance, unity. In all its developments it is "one and the selfsame Spirit" throughout. In the form of benevolence it may be felt for those in whom no delightful traits can be discovered. This was the Master's love for Jerusalem—sorrow for the sinner's guilt and compassion for his doom. As brotherly love, it unites the believer to all who have part with himself in the communion of the saints with God. Like the *knitting* of souls between David and Jonathan, Christian fellowship makes us one with all who belong to Christ, whether the militant on earth or the triumphant in heaven.

But the term *complacency* expresses the most exalted form of holy love. This speaks delight in the contemplation of what is truly lovely—delight in all the holy, created or uncreated—delight in all holiness and holy happiness. Even that commiserating love just mentioned springs from this delight, because it is pity for those who are strangers to such happiness. From thence this heart for all that is worthy of love passes on to become a living sympathy with the happiness of all who draw their joys from Christ—in other words, it becomes love to the brethren. These are but parts of the one complacent affection with which renewed souls gaze upon whatever is lovely, happy and holy throughout the universe, and which is consummated in love to Christ—love to God.

We have our highest view of it when we reflect upon its Source. It flows in the heart of God. The Holy Scriptures say of him, not merely that he is lovely and deserving of love, or that he is the Author and Dispenser of love, but they make of this grace one of the vitalities of his being: "God *is* Love. As when, assuming the expressive name, "I AM," he impersonated universal existence, so when we hear him proclaimed as one who is Love, we think of all existing loveliness as part and essence of himself. "He that dwelleth in love, dwelleth in God, and God in him." Even those awful attributes to which we ascribe his dealings of wrath are the necessary result of his complacency in holy happiness. If he had less delight in such happiness, he might be less severe against its hindering cause, sin.

In bringing us to become partakers of this grace, God incorporates in our spiritual natures an elementary portion of his own. He fills us with the fullness of himself, and we feel the new man within us to be a Divine effluence. To possess the love of God is to be *born* of God. The Holy Ghost sheds it abroad in our hearts, and then it affords us in our capacity such delight as it gives to God in his.

There is for the believer this peculiar joy in his apprehension of the love of God, that he feels it individualizing himself. It appears before him, not alone in the general aspect of a complacency in all that is good and happy, but his faith beholds in it the sentiment of his heavenly Father toward himself. It has been mentioned that longings for love are an instinct of the human heart, and also that only requited love yields pleasure. No complacency in others could answer the demand of our nature, while we felt that toward ourselves all were cold. The regenerate person carries into the new field for his affections all these desires to become the object of love. Indeed, in that new field these desires are intensified by his consciousness of the purer nature of that love which he now longs to receive.

And it is in this field that the yearnings of his spirit are met and filled. His view wanders delighted over the boundless extent of worlds and beings on which his heavenly Father smiles, but the thrilling experience of his heart is that of God's especial affection for himself. He is bowed in grateful humility and in wonder that the Majesty of the universe can draw so near to so mean a thing, while he listens to the testimony of the Spirit: "Since thou wast precious in my sight, thou hast been honorable and I have loved thee." It comes again —what joy dwells in the sound!—"I love them that love me." The Spirit who whispers this witness in his ear breathes it into his heart. Then he is satisfied with the reciprocity of affection between himself and God; and such love, meeting with such a requital, answers the highest demand of his new-born nature.

There is a point of still higher interest in God's particular regard for the believer. It belongs to the grand system which was formed for the recovery of a lost world. It comes in the death and intercession of the Redeemer, and through that death and intercession it is bestowed upon an unworthy but repentant sinner. Viewed in this light, it becomes the love of Christ. Before the cross all our thoughts of Divine love are tender and subduing. The atonement, through which the sinner becomes justified, blesses him with the first complacent smile of his Maker. His Redeemer's mediation presents him before the throne as an object of heavenly regard. The Holy Spirit's sanctifying work in his soul clothes him with those attributes of loveliness which win the Divine heart. He beholds his Saviour cheered amid his toils and trials, and sustained under the endurance of Divine wrath, by the consciousness that he was performing the highest labor of love: "Having loved his own which were in the world, he loved them unto the end." He listens, and all is made right and happy for himself and in himself, while he hears the ever-living intercession of Jesus for his friends—"that they might have *my joy* fulfilled in themselves; that *the love wherewith thou hast loved me* may be in them, and I in them."

This is God's own love. It is the well-spring of those streams which, flowing into the believer's soul, become his love, good and glorious in accordance with the goodness and glory of the Fountain which issues it. Faith is tranquilizing, happy and good. So is hope, and so is every grace. But "the greatest of these is Love."

# X.

## LOVE.

### SECOND—ITS SCOPE.

FIELDS for the range of holy affections are ever open. In no one of its manifestations can sanctified love become languid for the want of interesting objects upon which to bestow itself.

In this world the calls for our benevolence are incessant. The whole creation groans and travails in pain. High-handed wrong usurps the place of justice, and cruelty reigns where mercy should be enthroned. For all this God feels, and he will have us feel. Against this he directs the whole course of his active providence, and he expects us to labor as well as feel with himself.

The general misery which sin brings upon the world is made up of unnumbered instances of individual suffering. Multitudes of these are brought to our own door. The poor we have always with us. Around us the helpless are needing help, the desponding are asking for cheer, and the mourners are looking about for comfort. Pointing us to each call upon our benevolence, God informs us exactly how we may judge whether his own feeling for the children of sorrow dwells in our breasts. "Whoso hath this world's good, and seeth his brother have need, and shutteth up his bowels of compassion from him, how dwelleth the love of God in him!" The neglect of the offices of humanity is given as one decisive proof that the heart is a stranger to God. And we are to be weighed in the same balances at the final judgment. Christ, there enthroned as the arbiter of our eternal destinies, will exhibit the hungry, the thirsty, the houseless wanderer, the naked, the sick and the imprisoned—all those in whose cases love to himself should have been expressed—and the dread accusation against such as turned coldly from the sufferers will be, "Ye did it not to me."

Think, too, of the call for our compassion toward the enemies of God. The Divine heart bleeds over their infatuation. God's call to them is the mournful pleading of a father with a wandering son, whom he knows not how to abandon to profligacy and ruin. We behold the tears of the Redeemer for lost souls; we see, in the sorrows of his death, the evidence that all which he spoke was felt in his heart; and then we know how we must feel, and what we must do, if we share the spirit of Christ. We too must mourn over sinners who are rushing upon ruin. More than this, we must gird ourselves for cheerful self-denials, for warm personal effort and for a generous participation in every enterprise which is adapted to their recovery. And when was ever an opportunity wanting for the exercise of love to the brethren? This fraternal affection is, in a peculiar sense, the fruit of our Lord's dying love, and is hence proclaimed as the *new commandment* of the gospel. The special attraction which draws believers, *as such*, toward each other, seems to have been less distinctly felt under the previous dispensation, when the Jew loved his fellow Jew more on account of their national affinity than because they were heirs to the same heaven. In the New Testament we find the clearer recognition of brotherly love as created by our oneness in God. There we listen to that wondrous intercession of our Advocate, which disclosed some beauties of grace new to the world—"That they all may be one; as thou Father art in me, and I in thee, that they may be one in us; that the world may believe that thou hast sent me."

We often speak of "celestial fruits on earthly ground" and of "heaven begun below." In this experience of love to the brethren such a foretaste is well identified. Cold and sadly deficient in the best participations of grace is the soul of him who feels no thrill in the thought that

"The fellowship of kindred minds
Is like to that above."

In our daily walks we meet with those who are fellow-pilgrims to the city of God. Their hopes, their object of life, and their love, are the same as our own. We mourn the same sinfulness, we look to the same atonement, we rejoice in the same forgiveness, we burn with the same purified ambitions, and we live the same new life. These communings are the refreshing arbors along the steep of Christian toil, where the pilgrim reposes for a season and feels his brow fanned by the gales of heaven.

The delights of this fraternal love need not be so much marred, as we are apt to think they must be, by the imperfections of our fellow-Christians. Holy affection exhibits its glory and strength in triumphing over such causes of disturbance. Its influence over our hearts is then more observable, and more honorable to religion, than it probably would have been had it shined in no such darkness. When this celestial spirit is beheld walking into the arena of religious controversies or personal strifes, with their angry excitements, and stilling the tempest with the magic reflection, *Ye are brethren!* then the world beholds it armed with the strength of God and glowing in the beauty of heaven.

On this point the Church has not received the fair award of justice. She enjoys more of the happiness of brotherly love than her enemies credit her with—more even than her friends have always claimed for her. It is not denied that she has been rent by discords and sometimes deeply agitated by contending passions. For these sad outbreaks of moral obliquity much is due to men of no piety, deceivers and self-deceived, who have entered her visible organization and obtained her confidence. Their zeal for points or parties, even when furious, has been mistaken by others, and perhaps by themselves, for Christian attachment to principle. These are spots in our feasts of charity for which God will not, and men ought not to judge us, any farther than as we submit to their corrupt influence. Not a few who are, in the main, friends of Christ, are also implicated in these scenes of strife, and the reproach which has followed their influence cannot be denied.

But people forget that the discordant

aspects of the Christian family are always the most obvious, and most likely to be observed through a magnifying medium. The report of the bitter speech of one Christian against his fellow-disciple will spread for leagues, while the sweet expression of fellowship is often not heard beyond the room where it is spoken. The controversies of the true Church are, like the surgings of the sea, on the surface. Beneath them is a silent and smooth under-current, always of the same element and flowing in the same direction. The excitements of the first are occasional, often impulsive and always conspicuous. The last is the quiet flood of the river of God, less striking to the superficial observer, but for ever enjoyed. Every heart in which Divine love truly dwells flows in that flow and joins in the universal sentiment of the redeemed—one hope, one labor, one spirit, one Head and one home.

What anticipations are awakened by our present faint experience of this fellowship! Expecting the hour when the redeemed shall sing with the voice together, because they see eye to eye, how the earnest cry sometimes ascends, "Lord, why are thy chariots so long in coming? Why tarry the wheels of thy chariots?"

The crowning feature of this holy love is, that its scope embraces both earth and heaven. We have seen that it ranges delighted among the lovely ones of earth, whom we meet from day to day. But faith brings us into the presence of beings of infinitely superior worth, for there is no blemish in them, and our delight in them is unqualified. Communion with God seems, for the time, to remove our souls from earth to heaven. Among the spirits who fill that world are the great company of the redeemed, who were as we are, and who are as we soon shall be. There are some of our dearly beloved ones, who could not abide our slow steps and so hastened before us to glory. Hand in hand we performed our pilgrimage for a short season, and the remembrance of those communings prompts our souls to make frequent ascensions up the ladder of vision to the land of the immortals. We see their white robes; they seem to beckon us with their smile—

> "Come away to the skies,
> My beloved, arise;"

we listen to the music of their harps of gold; we behold their dwelling-place in light unapproachable and full of glory; and then we feel that our holy affections can never die for the want of something good to love.

The same faith brings us into the presence of angels, cherubim and seraphim, those morning stars which sang together, and those sons of God who shouted for joy when our world sprang into being.

They have enjoyed an existence of uninterrupted holiness; they have numbered ages of service in ministering to the honor of the throne of heaven; and they have found what is always to be found, even on this earth, growing felicity in each new hour of consecration.

There also we look upon that face which is the brightness of the Father's glory. The eye of faith, looking through the veil of sense, beholds now enough of Christ to excite strong yearnings for the unclouded view of him, "whom having not seen, we love; in whom though we see him not, yet believing we rejoice with joy unspeakable and full of glory." And there too is the self-existing Author of this unspeakable bliss, enjoying love, imparting love and himself *being* love. Surrounded by those throngs of the ransomed and those angelic "living ones," and having in himself all the gloriousness of the Father, the Jesus, Saviour, and the Holy Spirit, Sanctifier, he is the one everlasting object of contemplation upon which we may feast for ever.

Thus, in those hours when the soul shuts itself in from this world and looks through the glass of faith into that which is unseen and eternal, as the picture of an entire heaven offering itself to our love unrolls itself, presenting view after view, rising in interest and delight, our weak sight soon reaches the point beyond which it cannot go until we see as we are seen and know as we are known. But the present span of our vision is wide enough, and its aggregate of objects large enough, to suffice for any longing this side of heaven. Our spiritual arithmetic gives the numbers—Mount Zion, the city of the living God, the heavenly Jerusalem, the innumerable company of angels, the general assembly and church of the first-born, God the Judge of all, the spirits of just men made perfect, Jesus the Mediator of the new covenant, and the blood of sprinkling. We add up the column and the sum is *Love.*

Casting out all fear, filling our strongest yearnings for affection, incorporating our natures with the happy nature of God himself, clinging to us with a hold which neither death nor life nor any other creature of God can unloose, and enriching all its other blessings by constantly drawing us nearer to Calvary and Mount Zion, what a sanctuary for the soul is love! What light and blessings it sheds upon the hour when death shall loosen the soul for its flight to the home of all holy affection! The believer, led by its soft guidance, approaches the shore where he can hear the voices of the songs from beyond the river. They adore, they sing, they shout; but high above all, and through the eternal age, they LOVE.

# XI.

## THE SERVICE OF DOING.

### FIRST—INCITEMENTS.

THAT is a false religion which is laid hold of only for the sake of its hope for the world to come. There can be no greater mistake concerning the intent of the death of Christ toward the redeemed than to suppose it meant only for their deliverance from future misery. The grace which brings salvation does not subordinate God to us but us to him; and that is a selfish estimate of its meaning which would make it read, Everything *for* us: nothing *from* us. A lively hope of heaven is a fair result of vital religion—nothing more. The elementary feature of such religion—that without which it has no reality of existence—is *consecration.* Its possessor has made the solemn consecration of *himself* to God, and this consecration is for both worlds—the life that now is as well as the life to come. The moral condition of the world gives to this consecration a definite and tangible import. It brings it out from the region of abstract sentiment and places it in concrete relation to the work of God in the world. In direct terms it means *work.* Personal effort, such as devising, toiling, praying, giving, and all up to the point of such sacrifice of selfish interests as will be felt, is implied. Not merely first in *time*, but, all through life, first in *order* of effort, the Christian seeks the kingdom of heaven and its righteousness.

It lies in the nature of a true Christian consecration that this service should be a cheerful one. The whole life, its anxieties, ambitions, bent of activities and delight in the results of living, has taken its spirit from the cross. In the feeling inseparable from a true experience of grace from the cross, that "for me to live is Christ," the service in which consecration is carried out, rises from the character of a cold duty to a delightful aspiration for fellowship with Jesus. This view of it is peculiarly vivid in the light of his example. There is a motto for the Christian life in his words, "I must work the works of him that sent me while it is day; the night cometh when no man can work." He said this in his assumed human nature —the "form of a servant" which he "took upon himself"—a nature in which he could be felt by us as an example. It was a nature capable of toils; capable of feeling that they were toils; susceptible of their wearing influence upon manly energy and susceptible of the oppression of spirit which they sometimes produce. With him work was no less work than with us. Fatigue of body and faintness of spirit were as real with him as with us. With as full an experience of these things of humanity as was ever felt in this world, he expressed his sense of the life-long service due to the Father, and his purpose, as an appointed worker, whose task, like the task of a hireling, was set to work out his whole day, for the night was coming on.

True, it is not for us to do the *one great work* which was his more special mission in the world—that of dying a sacrificial death for the sins of men; but we are to work for the same great end—the salvation of sinners through that atonement. Our Lord has not called certain classes only of his redeemed friends into the activities of his service; he has left his example for all, giving to all the grace to do and spreading out work abundant for all. It may be found in the pulpit, the Sabbath-school, the parish, in supplying and sending forth ambassadors of the cross everywhere, among the neglected and suffering, in all the highways and byways of life, and in every appointed means for reforming and blessing the world. It is work which requires a surrender of carnal ease, toil, willing endurance and sometimes exposure to reproach, but it is work which cannot be put off without imperiling the hope of heaven. There is no exception to our Lord's everlasting law, "Whosoever doth not bear his cross, and come after me, cannot be my disciple." The toils and exposures under which our consecration to God lays us, are only sharing with Jesus the burdens of the service. When he spoke the words we have quoted, he recognized for himself no more constancy in duty than is binding on us, and mentioned no motive that does not apply, in its full strength, to our case. Works of as high and eternal interest as those which brought him to earth are set before us. To us also the night cometh—the night when no man can work.

We turn from the example of Jesus living in the world, to the power of his death in the believer. Reference has already been made to the fact that it bears just as explicitly upon a working, Christian life as upon the final blessedness of heaven. Cursory views of the grace of the cross generally pass over the first and rest upon the last of these results of the atonement in the believer. They look only for the crown and never for the cross. But a thoughtful view of our Lord's death sweeps the wider scope of its bearing and sees not only what it is to do for the pardoned sinner, but also what the love of Christ constrains that sinner himself to do for his fellow-sinners, and more especially for the Lord who died for him.

With New Testament saints, this last

was much the most prominent part of the theme of the cross. So Paul spoke his own experience of its power when he wrote of filling up, in his own flesh, that which is behind of the afflictions of Christ, for the sake of his body, which is the Church. In other words, he looked not upon Christ as the only sufferer in this great work of winning a church out of this apostate world to holiness and to heaven. Though his was the only true sacrificial work, still he left behind afflictions which his people were to fill up in their *flesh*—in some *outward* service of doing or enduring—in carrying out the purpose for which he died. They were to watch and work as their Master watched and worked, and sometimes also, like their Master, to suffer and die for the cause.

From men of that spirit, how noble would have been the utterance of our working song—

"Must Jesus bear the cross alone,
And all the world go free?
No, there's a cross for every one,
And there's a cross for me!"

From the stand-point of Calvary the writers of the New Testament were accustomed to look neither at earth with its toils, nor at heaven with its rest, by itself alone. "To this end Christ both died and rose and revived, that he might be Lord both of the dead and living." "We labor, that whether present or absent, we may be accepted of him." "For me to live is Christ, and to die is gain." Over and over again has the spirit of inspiration brought the warfare and the victory into the same field of vision, and in such terms as make the power of the cross no less direct toward a faithful Christian life than toward a triumphant death. So goes on our hymn—

"The consecrated cross I'll bear,
Till death shall set me free;
And then go home my crown to wear,
For there's a crown for me."

The shortness of the time comes in as a warning incentive, calling for earnestness of service. True it is not the holiest, and should not be the strongest spur to Christian activity. It is of use only in this inconstant world. In heaven, without any warnings for haste from dying chambers and funeral bells, they work faster and better than any of us here. The most prompt service is rendered where the incentive is the unmixed one of love. So, in his better moments, it is felt by the Christian in this world. It is not rare that the true lover of his unseen Lord enters into the feelings of the three disciples, who, on the Mount of Transfiguration, ravished by the sight of the excellent glory, spoke first of all their consecration to service. It is good to be here, if we may build tabernacles for thee and thine. It is good to dwell on the mount of love, if we may do the works of love.

Still, in commending to us inducements to service, God treats us as yet living in a world where the best frames of spirit are inconstant. It is earth yet, and so Death must stand forth our ordained preacher, filling all the ways of life with his sepulchral oratory, moving us to do with our might what our hands find to do, for the solemn reason that there is no work in the grave whither we go.

The best laborers in the Church might live too long. It is a painful thought, but with the records of human inconstancy before us, it cannot be suppressed. Short as the day of the hireling now is, we sometimes grow impatient of toil. The work for to-day is often laid aside until to-morrow; that which belongs to the present year is postponed until the next. This is done by those who know it may be at the sacrifice of the last opportunity for performance. What then might become of the industry of us all, if, in our present habitudes of body and mind, we were immortal? Is it not well for the kingdom of Christ in the world, that the great programme of labor through which its eventual triumph is to come passes from hand to hand? Is it not well that death is made one of the instrumentalities through which efficient service is perpetually secured? Each laborer is thus brought to feel that he has but a short time with his task before it is handed over to some successor. If he would do anything he must do it fast. If he would not carry the one thriftless talent in the napkin to the final judgment he must make haste to use it.

Any worldly enterprise which requires ages for its perfection feels the influence of death as an element of efficiency. The administration of an empire would become indolent if any one sovereign, even a Charlemagne, were immortal on his throne. In this world, it is the recognized law for all long successful enterprise, that while time impairs efficiency, freshness promotes the vigor of service.

The enterprise which Christ has left to his Church is not exempt from this rule. It is a work for ages. Long centuries of toil and suffering must be worked and suffered through, before reaching the final achievements of the cross in this world of sin. The vigor of service must not relax to the end. And so death passes the work along from hand to hand. It takes it from those whose ambition for toil is bowing under the burden, and hands it down to others, who, in fresh energy, are panting to play their glorious part.

This arrangement, so good for the Church, has no ungenerous aspect toward the individual. The sentinel on his weary watch listens without dread for the bell which strikes the hour for another to take his round. So with the servant of

Jesus, faithful at his post: why should he recoil from the approaching hour for exchanging the watch? Why should he linger at nightfall, reluctant to leave his work, when his good Redeemer would have him look through the darkness to the rewarding morning? All will go well, whether with himself or with the work he leaves. Men die, but the cause of redemption lives, and shall never want men to bear it on while one sinner remains under the day of grace.

This view of the Divine wisdom in the uses of death, speaks, oh how solemnly! to the writer and reader, to the whole company of the Church, to all who have any thought of reaching heaven. Its voice is, Work! Work for Christ and for human salvation! Work while it is day! and remember that the day is not done until the sun is fully set. What can be better for the Christian veteran than to march in his panoply up to the very gate of heaven! What better than to have it said of him when he is gone—

> "Thou hast fallen in thine armor,
> Thou servant of the Lord;
> Thy last breath crying, Onward!
> Thy hand upon thy sword!"

There follows naturally the thought of this further incitement to a faithful service of doing—its intimate connection with the glory to come. No careful reader of the Holy Scriptures can have failed to notice how often they connect the labor with the reward—the cross with the crown. So our Lord strengthened in his personal followers zeal for action and faith for endurance: "Ye are they which have continued with me in my temptations; and I appoint unto you a kingdom, as my Father hath appointed unto me." The voice from heaven to the Revelator in Patmos, bade him write concerning the blessed dead who die in the Lord, that they "rest from their labors, and their works do follow them." Without here pausing over the theological relation of the works to the reward, no one can carefully read either of the passages just quoted without receiving from them this plain impression—there must be first toil for Christ on earth and then repose with him in heaven. The hand that has clung longest to the cross lays the firmest grasp upon the crown. It is as true in holy activities and rest as in our physical aptitudes, that "the sleep of the *laboring man* is sweet." It was written of those who amid great tribulation had washed their robes in the blood of the Lamb. "*Therefore*, [because of what they did and experienced on earth,] are they before the throne of God, and serve him day and night in his temple. . . . The Lamb which is in the midst of the throne shall feed them, and shall lead them unto living fountains of waters, and God shall wipe away all tears from their eyes."

See how the faithful and honored servants of Christ have, from the threshold of glory, looked back upon their life-work for Jesus! Paul, when an old and war-scarred soldier of Jesus, with his weary feet almost on the immortal shore, wrote in happy review of all he had done and suffered for his Lord, and of the intimate connection between his toils and endurances and the joyous triumph which awaited him. "I am now ready to be offered, and the time of my departure is at hand. I have fought a good fight, I have finished my course, I have kept the faith: henceforth there is laid up for me a crown of righteousness which the Lord, the righteous Judge, shall give me at that day."

Thus stretching his view over earth behind and heaven before—a view which embraced the whole bearing of the endurance upon the triumph—he sent back his voice to the young laborer, to whom he thus wrote to work for Christ: "Thou therefore endure hardness as a good soldier of Christ."

The writer of these pages many years ago visited an aged friend—one who had done long service for Christ and who was then suffering and sinking under mortal disease and expecting soon to die. He had reached the point where he felt that his earthly service was closing, and his longing gaze was turned intensely toward heaven. From those beamings of glory he looked back once more to earth and to the Christian's work on the earth. "Oh," said he, "I have loved it, but I never before had such views of the inexpressible joy of laboring for God. I want to say to you; I want to say to all the ministers; yes, I want to lift up a loud voice and say to all the brethren, ministers or laymen, Work for God! work, work! I have no words to tell you how blessed it is. Tell them that they will never know until they view it from where I now stand, but they will know it all then."

The order of a gallant naval captain, "Don't give up the ship!" was immortalized because it was spoken in death. So let the shout of the dying Christian veteran be passed along the hosts, the rallying cry for fresh encounters with sin and Satan in this world of ours, Work while it is day! work for God!

# XII.

## THE SERVICE OF DOING.

### SECOND—ENCOURAGEMENTS.

THE most real trials of Christian effort do not consist in their tax upon our means and strength. *Discouragement* is the chief foe to heartsome labor. The holding of that scowling fiend at bay is always an indispensable condition of happiness, and generally of usefulness, in our work.

A sincere but too easily depressed Christian writes to his friend: "God knows that I have no greater desire than to see that I am really doing good in his cause. I would labor for it; for this I would gladly spend and be spent; I do not know that it would be too much to say that I would willingly die for it. But my courage is almost broken and I am sorely tempted to give up. It is not that I crave rest. I am not tired of work. I took the toil into account when I gave myself to Christ. I was warned to expect it, and I did so. I not only expected it, but I sought it. I have no difficulty with what some would call the *drudgery* of the service. In truth that is rather exhilarating than disheartening. I have noticed the flush of exultation with which a boy brings his first harvest-sheaves to the pile which his father is gathering. He pants under his work, but he is full of joy because it is his own contribution of effort in support of his father's interest. I can comprehend his pleasure, and, if other things were right, I would enjoy a similar feeling in all my labors to gather fruit unto life eternal. The exacting of mere means and energies in this work offers the least of all temptations to the repining propensity. It is only the trial which self-denial and fatigue give to patience; and that is with me the mildest form of discipline for this virtue.

"'Tired of *work?*' No indeed! But these dark skies—what *do* they mean? Will the sun never break through the clouds in the moral heavens? In the harness of mere *toil* I could work on to old age, happy to live and to die, but I sink under *discouragement.* When I see that my hands are stretched forth all the day long to a disobedient and gainsaying people; when I see that, after all is done, the moral changes are apparently against the cause of Christ and iniquity is actually gaining ground, and that even the tender ear of childhood is turned away from the story of the love of Jesus, thus making the prospect for the future worse and worse, I find it almost impossible to listen to the voice which says, 'Persevere and hope on!' I know how wicked despondency is, but when it comes upon me as an armed man, I have no strength left for the battle. I sink in the deep waters: God help me!"

The above complaint is an example of many which go up from the field of Christian toil. Men of really devoted spirit are not always courageous when they see the world growing harder in the very face of their labors, and especially when long continued efforts still bring few satisfactory results. They would keep better watch against despondency if they would more carefully observe its tendency toward acrimony of spirit. They are prone to indulge angry feelings toward men for whose good they labor, but who ungratefully resist every benign influence which is employed in their behalf. They are apt to lose patience with others who profess to be devoted to the same noble interest which fills their own hearts, but who are never found at the post of duty when their personal services are most needed.

But worse than this, when the Christian laborer feels his hope of success giving away, he sometimes carries his displeasure against God himself. Before he is aware he finds himself dissatisfied —shall it be said angry?—because God suffers men to remain unmoved and does not openly honor his efforts to promote the glory of Christ in the world. Like the prophet under the juniper tree, first discouraged and then vexed, he is ready to cry, "It is enough; now, O Lord, take away my life." Like the same prophet in the cave, his heart adopts the petulant expostulation that, while he has been very jealous for the Lord God of hosts, he has been ungenerously deserted of heaven and left alone in his work.

This is the natural culminating point of all discouragement under Christian labor. And when this point is reached we can see what a vile as well as gloomy thing such discouragement is. It is a quarrel with heaven, and it must be given up. It may cost long and hard struggle with the morbid habit of spirit, but it must be given up. Otherwise there is no cheer for toil, perhaps no good in it, certainly no heavenly peace for the life, and who can be sure of any precious hope in death?

Suppose then we look over this broad field of the service of doing, first inquiring what belongs to us and what to God. Let us see whether what we so often call the unfruitfulness of Christian labor may not be a delusion of the outward sense, and whether the despondency arising from it is not often the self-will of a mind which assumes to itself the prerogative of shaping means and ends. It is certain that no cloud of real gloom can abide over any true service for Christ, and there are standpoints of vision from which we can see the mists passing off and all such service glowing under the promise, "Your labor is not in vain in the Lord."

Here is one thought to lift the cloud: God has nowhere promised to reward us for the *success* of our efforts. He has never spoken of their *results* as the thing for which he bestows upon us his approval. The spirit and character of these efforts is one thing: the effect which they accomplish another. They are entirely distinct, and each is to be viewed by itself. One involves our personal responsibility, while God alone takes care of the other. The assurance that we shall be blessed in all our toils and sufferings for the cause of Christ has only these uniform and simple conditions, that we are to do our best, and do it under the incitement of love. This closes the whole account of what concerns us.

Then when our Lord looks smilingly

upon us, as he looked upon the loving disciple of whom he said, "She hath done what she could," we may be happy under those smiles without waiting to learn what use he will make of the things done. Whether the crop freshens in the showers of spring and ripens under the harvest sun, or whether it seems as if perished in the frosts of winter or drought of summer, there remains a blessing for the faithful sower of the seed, which, to his own soul at least, shall be a harvest reward: "God is not unrighteous to forget your work and labor of love which ye have showed toward his name." However men may speak of toiling to no purpose, his word of encouragement is never withdrawn. The Christian, whose trusting soul looks up to the crown of life as one certain prize for those who are simply *faithful* unto death, has no trembling for the issue. Though now worn and tempted to faint under watchings, apparently almost in vain, for some present tokens of usefulness, this refreshing thought makes him once more happy in his toil,—that if he is faithful for Christ's sake, a few hours more of work will bring the welcome change. A few hours more, and

> "There on a green and flowery mount
> Our weary souls shall sit,
> And with transporting joy recount
> The labors of our feet."

He may well be "steadfast, unmovable, always abounding in the work of the Lord" whose strong faith is anchored to the assurance, "forasmuch as ye know that your labor is not in vain in the Lord."

But it is not alone this anticipation of the heavenly reward which makes our present service cheerful and satisfying. Irrespective of present success, all that we do in faithful love brings present recompense to our hearts. Christian work has always its reflex bearings upon the worker, which become the heart's

"Celestial fruit on earthly ground"—

foretastes of the recompense to come. The "doer of the work" is "blessed *in his deeds.*" Good reason may exist why God's open approbation of our service should linger, but he hastens the visits of his love to our souls. Indeed, on a careful examination of his discipline of our hearts, we shall sometimes be surprised to find the best spiritual comforts arising from the very things which are darkest to our senses.

Look for example at the power of what men call cross-providences and causes for despondency to excite the confiding Christian's *faith.* This is a joyous grace—one of the celestial three which are stars of the first magnitude in the firmament of Christian peace. It is evidence of pardon; it unites to Christ; it is one medium through which we look up and see the Blessed One. Faith is eyes to the believer, "for we walk by faith, not by sight."

But without some sensual darkness there can be no faith. The things of which it is the evidence are *not seen.* The good of which it is the substance is *hoped for*—meaning, of course, *not now possessed.* If we could now see everything take the form in which our infirm policy would have shaped it, what room would remain for the refreshing sentiment of *trust* which keeps us so near to Christ? But as it is, God's ways are so inscrutably above human policies, and his paths in such a deep sea, that much of our joy in him grows out of that inwrought confidence which tells us that all done by our heavenly Father is well done. Whatever awakens faith becomes tributary to our delight.

Then it is not strange if our covenant

Lord leads us along dark paths that he may teach our trembling hearts the blessing of trust. Perhaps for this very reason he purposely withholds from our sight the reward which, for the present, he wishes only the eye of faith to behold. What we call the discouragement of expending our charities and efforts only to see things grow worse and worse, may then be a Divine culture of the grace which draws the believer near to God, to wait under the shadow of his throne for the chosen hour when we shall be allowed to see, as well as believe, that all went on well. In this spirit Cowper wrote of the "mysterious way" in which God moves, "his wonders to perform:"

"Judge not the Lord by feeble sense,
But trust him for his grace;
Behind a frowning providence
He hides a smiling face.

"His purposes will ripen fast,
Unfolding every hour;
The bud may have a bitter taste,
But sweet will be the flower.

"Blind unbelief is sure to err,
And scan his works in vain;
God is his own interpreter,
And he will make it plain."

But faith is not the only reflex comfort of toiling under outward gloom with a true and fond devotion to Christ. *Obedience* is a source of joy. There is an inexpressible sweetness in the reflection that we are striving to do the will of God. This sentiment, when sincerely cherished, is nothing less than the spirit of Christ in the soul. We look up to our Lord, and we hear him proclaim the moving cause of his own mission of toil and suffering in the world—"Lo! I come; in the volume of the book it is written of me, I delight to do thy will, O my God!" Sustained by the happy consciousness that he was faithful to an appointed work, his courage did not give way in those dark hours when even his own received him not. He knew that his labors were accomplishing the Divine purpose, and he was satisfied.

Like him we are sent into the world to do the will of our Father in heaven. It is a holy mission which we are to execute—not to acquire a personal reputation for effective talent, but for the glory of him who sent us. Whatever amount of success may now attend our labors, we shall soon "give account with joy," if, with the consciousness of honest purpose and after faithful endurance, we can say to God, as we ascend, "I have finished the work which THOU gavest me to do."

# XIII.

## THE SERVICE OF DOING.

### THIRD—FRUIT.

MENTION has been made of the blessedness of Christian service, irrespective of the question of outward success. Let it not however be inferred that we may be careless respecting the visible fruit of our labors or cherish anything less than a deep solicitude concerning the persons or things which are the objects of them. When allowed to reap with joy a quick harvest from what was sown in tears, we are indeed blest with the peculiar favor of our rewarding God. If we are permitted to behold the waste places of the earth robing themselves with the glory of Lebanon and the excellency of Carmel and Sharon, under our cultivation, our hearts should contribute their own happy strains to the voice of joy and singing which rises from the reclaimed desert.

On the other hand, the want of visible tokens of success should always awaken solemn inquiry why so little harvest grows under so much culture. Every class of laborers—ministers or laymen, those who speak, write, pray, work or contribute of their worldly wealth—should each alike be faithful and resolute to reach the truth in such a scrutiny. It is always satisfying to reflect that we have done what we could for Christ. But this satisfaction would be a spurious peace if it produced indifference respecting the effect of our exertions.

The question, whether the impoverished state of the ground which we are striving to improve, may not be traced to our thriftless husbandry, is natural and pertinent. Others will make such an inquiry respecting us, and we ought to make it for ourselves. Have our efforts been uniformly obedient to the motions of the Holy Spirit in our hearts? Have we gone forth bearing precious seed, because we desired to reap a harvest, not for ourselves, for a party or for any human interest, but for God? While bestowing our diligence, were our hearts before the throne of grace in earnest prayer that God would do his own work? Have our plans been wise and our means appropriate? Has our patience been constant and our spirit affectionate? In the amount as well as spirit of our industry, have we been faithful, remembering the motive which so deeply affected our Master, "I must work the works of him that sent me while it is day; the night cometh when no man can work?"

Grave this on the memory as with the point of a diamond, that every Christian comfort requires some definite and intelligible evidence that we are proper subjects of it. Questions like the above must have a satisfactory answer in our consciousness before we can review what are called discouraging labors with perfect calmness. But when, looking over all this ground, we can say to the honor of Divine grace, that our hearts are clear or our short-comings forgiven, then peace will fly to our bosoms, however success may linger. We have done our part, and like our Divine Pattern, we find our delight in performing the will of God.

But there are yet richer words of cheer for the fainting toiler in the Christian field. All along God does support him with other promises besides the assurance of being himself watered from the river of heavenly love. All along there shines before him the pledge of everlasting truth, that faithful Christian effort shall accomplish valuable results in other hearts and promote the interest of Christ in the world. He has the assurance of heaven that he *is* doing good. It is written: "He that reapeth receiveth wages, and *gathereth fruit* unto life eternal, that both he that soweth, and he that reapeth, may rejoice together." "They that sow in tears shall reap in joy. He that goeth forth and weepeth, bearing precious seed, shall doubtless come again rejoicing, bringing his sheaves with him." Words of loving kindness and inspiring hope! And they are examples of a long array of like precious promises, in the light of which the shamefulness of such terms as *gloomy prospects* and *unrequited toil* is glaringly exposed. The care of heaven will nourish every seed, and bring forth in their best seasons, the blade, the ear, and after that, the full corn. THERE IS NO DARK PROSPECT IN THE DISCHARGE OF DUTY.

Our notions of success are apt to be

earthly. We forget that there are other worlds which form the theatre where great events are accomplished. We measure time by days and years, and from thence we obtain our ideas of the fast and the slow. When the wheels of providence seem, in our impatient view, to turn lazily, we forget that they are moving in an eternal journey. They will take their time, it is true, but they will never stop. The comprehensiveness of the government of God—what a reviving theme to the faithful workers for Christ! The path in which THE ETERNAL walks is the way everlasting. It can never be sought out by malign counter-agencies. "The vulture's eye hath not seen it; the lion's whelps have not trodden it, nor the fierce lion passed by it." The same Omniscience which marks out the means keeps a sleepless watch for the end. Events which belong to each other may long wander apart, each fulfilling for a season some peculiar mission of its own; but their tracks will converge at the proper time. Causes and effects will meet whenever the great universal arrangement will be promoted by making their relation apparent. Then, but not before, we shall know what good we have done. The time may come soon or it may delay for ages, but it will come.

As God has just the hour and place for our efforts, so he has just the result which he expects and just the period which is propitious for its accomplishment. It may be our mission to ameliorate some special cases of human suffering, to exert a holy influence in the circle of home, to train some instruments of future usefulness, to promote some specific reformation, to lead sinners around us to Christ, to promote the general prosperity of the Redeemer's kingdom, to lay foundations upon which beneficent structures may rise in the future, or to exemplify the general principles of the Divine glory. On the uniform condition of faithfulness, success is assured to our peculiar mission, whatever it is. But the nature of that success, with the times and seasons, is in the hands of Him for whom we work. Our impatience cannot affect his far-reaching appointments. But our faith in his particular and universal providence arms us against despondency, and our long tasks are lightened by the thought that the achievement is sure.

We do not stop to perplex ourselves with the questions, *when?* and *where?* We hear from the voice of God all which properly concerns us: "In the morning sow thy seed, and in the evening withhold not thy hand." We then comfort our souls with the reflection that "our judgment is with the Lord and our work with our God." We are satisfied with the Divine approval. We feel a sweet consciousness that we are spending and being spent for Christ. Our consciences are at peace and our souls are ennobled by the thought that we are God's own chosen instruments of good—polished shafts in his quiver.

One* who had labored faithfully, and with many prayers, as a lay exhorter, beheld year after year pass with scarcely a cheering ray of present success. His field was one of the most forbidding which exist in Christian lands. He was derided in the streets, religion was scorned and the name of Christ was hourly blasphemed. Friends urged him to give over. They told him he had made a fair trial of the power of the

* For this narrative, the writer is indebted to the remote memory of the reading of his boyhood, the period when the impression of narratives is enduring. He believes it was read from a London paper, but at this period he can give no voucher for either its source or its truthfulness. In the kingdom of grace it has too many parallels to be regarded as incredible, and therefore serves the purpose of an illustration, whether the reader accept it as historical or as a parable.

gospel among those reprobates, and that was enough.

But in his earnest communion with Heaven he obtained some peculiar promise—an inwrought token from the Angel of the covenant. For who will say that God makes no special communications of this kind to those who are placed by himself where their support is peculiarly needed? To every proposal that he should abandon his field he replied that he was more and more convinced that he was doing work for God and he must not leave it.

Death arrested these labors. He had seen little outward appearance of good, but he did not mourn over an hour of his self-denying service as wasted labor. The *special token* cheered his last heavenly communion this side of the veil, and he departed under the feeling, not only that he had performed service which, for Christ's sake, would be accepted, but that he had done a great work. Was this peculiar assurance to which his faith anchored itself visionary? Was it all a dream that "a cake of barley tumbled into the host of Midian," smiting the tents of the uncircumcised? or was it indeed "the sword of Gideon, the son of Joash, a man of Israel," into whose hand God had delivered those armies?

A young man who applied for ecclesiastical authority to go forth as an ordained minister of Christ was required to relate his religious experience. In so doing, he traced his conversion to the instrumentality of that lay exhorter. During the life of that faithful servant of Christ this youth had been one of the scorners who afflicted his soul. His death awakened him to solemn reflections. He reviewed his self-denying consecration, his tears of compassion and labors of love; he thought of his prayers that God would forgive those who despitefully used him—thought of all, until the remembrance of that example of Christian tenderness was too much to bear. He was brought to the cross, qualified for the ministry and sent forth to preach the everlasting gospel.

Not a moment was wasted in seeking an eligible post of labor. *There was but one place for him.* Who so well as himself could tell his late companions in wickedness how they had together sinned against the love of God, in sinning against the love of the self-denying servant of God? They listened with gradually improving decency, and at length with earnest attention. Some hearts bled under the same self-reproach which had broken his own. There were soon enough for a concert of prayer. Then, though the earlier day of grace had been despised, they asked of the Lord rain in the time of the latter rain, and he made bright clouds and gave them showers of rain. The dens of blasphemy were exchanged for places of prayer, and men whose garments had been clotted with each other's blood, in street brawls, sat together as exemplary rulers in the congregation of the saints.

After a few years of such service that young pastor followed the lay exhorter to glory. The reaper had received the wages, and gathered the eternal fruit. But oh the joy unspeakable and full of glory with which he that sowed and he that reaped rejoiced together!

# XIV.

## THE SERVICE OF SUFFERING.

### FIRST—THE CONSECRATION AND THE COVENANT.

A CHRISTIAN minister, in the seventy-seventh year of his age, was laid for several months upon a bed of suffering, and, as it proved in the end, the bed of death. He was a faithful and holy man, remarkable for an industrious discharge of the numerous duties which his somewhat peculiar position placed in his way. He had been wonderfully favored in relation to bodily health. One man out of a thousand could not be found who had enjoyed a freedom so uniform from sickness or other physical infirmities. He had often said that he hardly knew what pain was. It came however in those last months of his life, and wrought upon him with a terrible severity, as if it was resolved to balance his account with human suffering before he should be relieved for ever.

During that long season of distress his soul lay submissively in the Everlasting Arms. He spoke of God's dealings with quiet satisfaction, and of the Divine government with exceeding joy. "When," said he, "I consecrated myself to God I bound myself to *service.* Since then I have attached great importance to doing the will of God. Times occurred when it seemed hard, but it was part of the service, and I said to myself, *Do it.* But somehow it never until now struck my mind with much force that there is just as much service in *suffering* as in *doing* the will of God. I find it harder to suffer than to do his will; but I am just as truly in his work, and I believe that, for Christ's sake, he will accept the service of suffering as well as that of doing."

What a beautiful frame of mind for the Christian, pressed down with anguish of body and expecting no relief except in death! What an all-supporting sentiment in the hour of trial! What sublimer thought could be summoned to aid the soul struggling to bear itself above the angry waters!

The sufferer turned his thoughts back to the self-consecrating engagements of long past years. He remembered that many weary hours of toil had been lightened by the reflection that they were a part of the contract between his soul and Christ. He had experienced great joy in the belief that they would be accepted as acts of faithfulness to his engagement. It was not because he expected God to look upon him as righteous for these things, or because he trusted to anything short of the mediation of the

Redeemer for mercy and acceptance. Still, like Paul, he had labored that he might be accepted of him, and the hope of that acceptance had inspired his ambition to spend and be spent. Now he is brought into another department of duty still more trying, and, lo! these same covenant engagements come to his aid, armed with new strength to cheer and support. What a weapon of defence for holding distress at bay! He had bound himself to service, and it was his delight to fill out the engagement. He had served in the field, and now he was serving in the fire. It was service still, and the service of suffering would be no less acceptable than that of doing.

How strangely some of the most common truths float through the mind—known indeed to be real, but *perceived* only as shadows—until some event brings them into action as articles of experience! Then how we are astonished that things so old are yet so new—that though we seemed to have known them so long we did not know them at all! The new thought of the aged minister did not probably embrace any addition to his theoretical knowledge of the Christian life. But there was a point which had lain in the mind as a dim, shadowy, abstract thing, until the providence of God called him to take it up as emphatically *the* point for the present emergency. Then it burst upon his faith with all the freshness of a new revelation from heaven. Hitherto he had remembered how it was meat and drink to the Saviour to do the will of him that sent him; and he had made it the highest aspiration of his own renewed soul to do the will of God. But he had laid an emphasis on the word *do* which prevented him from seeing the comprehensiveness of the duty required. The true meaning of the word, as he afterward found, was to *yield obe-*

*dience;* and as Christ's obedience was rendered alike in preaching, healing and in suffering on the cross, so he could fulfill his covenant of service and perform the Divine will as really in the endurance of his bodily pains as in active labors for God. He could not be happy without serving God. He discovered that in suffering he could serve him as devotedly as ever, and he was happy.

This view of the Christian's endurance of suffering of whatever kind as a covenant service becomes more vivid as we reflect upon the condition on which he first gave himself to Christ. It was an act of consecration. The surrender was without limit. It embraced himself, body and soul, but it embraced more. All the circumstances which are to affect his condition, all future personal allotments, with whatever joys or sorrows await them, were included in the cheerful dedication of all to Christ.

Still more to the purpose is this consideration: not only did he, on his part, commit all his circumstances, with himself, to Christ, but in the covenant under which he was redeemed, those circumstances were placed by the Father under the special control of the Mediator of the covenant.

It is not enough to say of Christ that he is the mediatorial King of *the Church* which he bought with his own blood. In this office, he must needs have power so to adjust the events of *the world* that they shall promote the peace of his friends and lead to their sanctification, and to the final triumph which is mutually theirs and his own. This is one glory of the arrangement by which God "hath put *all things* under his feet, and given him to be head over all things *to the Church*"—for the Church's sake.

In this connection it should also be remembered that it is a prominent object of our Redeemer's mediatorial administration to afford his friends every desirable security from present evils, and to confer the greatest happiness which they are prepared to enjoy. Immeasurably blessed himself in the work which he finished upon the cross, he delights to impart the full benefit of that work to those for whose sake he sanctified himself. Under the covenant, he rules in providence as well as grace. Thus he is enabled to compel all things to "*work together* for good to them that love God." Here there is protection from present evils and support under present sorrows, as well as a future home where tears are wiped from all faces. Stretching its shadow over the whole path of Christian experience, from the hour of our espousals to the unending future, how truly this covenant makes of Christ

"Our refuge from the stormy blast,
And our eternal home!"

Once more, and with peculiar attention, be it remembered that if our peace under this covenant depends upon Christ's ability to overrule every event for our benefit, we could not withhold any one of the *all things* of ours from his control without destroying his power to make them work together for our good. If we would have the peace which the covenant promise secures to the submissive heart, we must cheerfully commit our circumstances to covenant control. The afflicted Christian, tempted out of the anguish of his spirit to become rebellious, and to say in relation to anything, "I cannot submit myself to the disposal of God, but I must have my own way," would rob Christ of the power of securing his happiness from every providential allotment.

But in the sweet consciousness that we are yielding all to the care of him who governs the world for the happiness of his people, we are prepared to rejoice in all our tribulations. Perfect consecration teaches the consoling power of the truth that "all things are for your sakes." Then our souls sit in the sanctuary of THE COMFORTER, and our sorrows are turned into a joy which no man taketh from us.

Such views of the dominion of our mediatorial King clear the darkened skies. It is true afflictions are afflictions still, but they are no longer the food for gloomy thoughts. They afford some of the best illustrations of the tenderness of God's heart and the sustaining power of his grace. There are indeed many mysterious dispensations which are never explained in this world. But they are justified in the eye of that faith which supports the Christian, when all other ground sinks beneath his feet. There is always a light in which they can be viewed, not merely without gloom, but with real satisfaction. There is always some explicit reason for rejoicing that God has not arranged matters as we should probably have ordered them, but has, in covenant goodness, ordained for us those light afflictions of a moment which work an exceeding and eternal weight of glory.

# XV.

## THE SERVICE OF SUFFERING.

### SECOND—THE SUBMISSION OF FAITH.

IN this world the outward condition is not the test of character. God has not marked the distinction between his friends and his enemies by a palpable contrast in their earthly comforts. The seventy-third Psalm records how one good but distressed man almost lost his faith, when he saw the righteous suffer while the wicked seemed only to prosper, and how nobly he recovered himself.

Affliction is the common lot. It is a war in which, like that with death, there is no discharge. The good and the bad are alike subject to the vicissitudes of wealth and poverty, honor and detraction, ease and pain, life and death. The best friends of God may sit at scant tables, with no provision for another repast except the unfailing promise that they shall be fed. They may be herded in uncomfortable abodes. They may see their children reach and pass the years when they need opportunities for improvement, from which poverty debars them. They may be mortified by the inconstancy of friendships professed in better days, and may receive inhumanity and wrong from men who do not fear to oppress them because they are too weak to resist.

In the abode of prayer, where every chamber is hallowed by delightful communion with heaven, a diseased sufferer pines away the long years. For her the morning sun rises and the evening shadows gather almost in vain. Freshening springs and golden autumns have no joy, because they bring no change to the weary monotony of pain.

In another domestic group, whose course has been marked with peculiar devotion to Christ, death has appeared, and, so far as regards this world, the purest light of earthly bliss is quenched for ever. True, in all sanctified sorrow, the wounds of earthly bereavement are healed by the Great Physician, but the mourner often remains scarred for life. Who has not known what it is to behold some of the precious affections of life hidden in sepulchral darkness? Past whose lips has the cup gone untasted?

> "There is no flock, however well attended,
> But one dead lamb is there;
> There is no household, howsoe'er defended,
> But has one vacant chair."

There is one theological truth which comes kindly to the aid of the sufferer who stands appalled before such pictures of human experience. It is not a deep thesis for the Reviews, but a peace-working doctrine for the plain Christian who, in his hour of anguish, is tempted to cry. What is my unpardonable sin that I am thus singled out for the judgment of God? The point is that of the distinction between sorrows that are simply *providential occurrences* in God's government, and those which are *retributive.* This distinction separates the *natural evils* to which sin exposes the human race at large, from those peculiar displays of the Divine wrath which are the proper *penalty* of sin, and which are measured out with strict regard to personal character. The truth is clear to calm thought, but in the hour of inward tumult it is sometimes forgotten, and when forgotten the refuge of trust fails.

It is not meant that sin does not bring our troubles upon us. On the contrary, let it never be overlooked that affliction is the fruit of sin—the consequence of living in a world of guilt, of which our own sin forms a part. Hence it is always a call to repentance. Forgetting this fact, we should fail to receive one of the solemn impressions of the atrociousness of rebellion against God. We do well to study the enormity of sin in every lesson by which God teaches the awful truth.

But these terrestrial troubles are not the *prescribed penalty* of transgression as written down in the law. Though they are the *fruit*, they are not the *punishment* of crime. For the believer is already justified by the work of his Redeemer. No part of a legal judgment or sentence of *condemning* wrath can be executed on those who are in him. "There is therefore now *no condemnation* to them which are in Christ Jesus." The justified person may partake largely of the trials of life as the general effect of sin, but of that which is appropriately the cup of *penal* wrath he can drink no more for ever. From the lips of the believer the dying Saviour snatched this chalice, and pressed it to his own. Then, while we must feel that sin is the instrument of all our human woes, we may nevertheless welcome the thought to our hearts that God may sometimes grieve us most while he loves us with his warmest love. Beyond the hiding of his face for a moment in a little wrath, we may look to the everlasting kindness with which the Lord our Redeemer will have mercy on us.

But beyond their share of natural evils, as partners in the common humanity, the servants of God sometimes experience other tribulations, more severe to human view, which grow directly out of their faithfulness to Christ. This was the form of discipline to which our Lord summoned the sons of Zebedee, and some measure of it is meted out to all his friends: "Ye shall drink indeed of my cup, and be baptized with the baptism that I am baptized with." The cruel mockings and scourgings and terrible martyrdoms of the ancient worthies were not the ordinary sufferings of humanity, but the peculiar dispensation of Heaven toward its own inheritors. Such forms of discipline vary with the ever-varying state of human affairs. But some peculiar trials for our Master's sake are provided for every age, and they must be accepted by all who will accept Christ himself.

It must not, however, be inferred that the griefs of the friends of Christ are heavier than those which the wicked endure. Sinners also have sorrows of their own, besides their participation of the calamities which are common to all. If Elijah, as a man of God, had in that character some special afflictions, what were they beside the peculiar troubles of Ahab as the enemy of heaven? The sorrows of Paul at the block, or Ignatius in the amphitheatre, were as a feather compared with the leaden woes concealed under the imperial robes of Nero or Trajan. The riot of the wicked passions is often the immediate cause of the most awful outward judgments which are felt this side of the infernal world. Remorse, the undying worm, gnaws the poor sinner's conscience, and his spirit is wearied out in the warfare with an angry God.

But here is the chief point of contrast. While there are sorrows common to all, and also peculiar tribulations for each class of men, the one receives a peculiar support, while the other has no refuge from the storm. The sinner battles with his troubles helpless and alone, and must be crushed by them in the end. But in the furnace the spirit of the friend of Christ is sustained by the faith that, in his case, God is refining the gold—that he is not pouring out his fury upon an enemy, but he is chastening whom he loves.

While the ploughers make long their furrows upon his back, a voice which was never whispered in the ear of an ungodly sufferer breathes like the melody of seraphim in his soul: "Ye now therefore have sorrow, but I will see you again, and your heart shall rejoice, and your joy no man taketh from you." "O thou afflicted, tossed with tempest, and not comforted! . . . the mountains shall depart and the hills be removed, but my kindness shall not depart from thee, neither shall the covenant of my peace be removed. . . . This is the heritage of the servants of the Lord." Appropriating to ourselves this comfort from the lips of our Lord, sorrow ceases to disturb our peace.

How incomparably superior to the highest human consolation is this heavenly comfort! The resignation of the man of the world to his troubles is the submission of philosophy. It is self-taught and self-sustained. Its availability depends wholly upon his mental fortitude. This submission claims to accomplish nothing more than a still patience under suffering. It never contemplates a happy reconciliation. The language of such a submission is, "Evils which cannot be avoided should be quietly borne. Outcries do not alleviate suffering. The noble nature of man ought to be strong to endure. None but cowards faint in the day of trouble. Since that which is laid upon us is an inevitable destiny, let us dignify ourselves by scorning to repine." In homelier phrase, such philosophical resignation is just this, all told: "What can't be cured must be endured."

To one who is strengthening his nerves for this submission to fate we say, Take your philosophy: we choose to fall back on the sublime principle of faith in God. The language of implicit trust in the aid of heaven is the tongue in which we will speak our triumph over trial, and tell of the clear shining before which the showers flee. In our troubles we cannot stop at the cold maxim that we must endure what cannot be helped, for under the teaching of Christ we have better learned why we are afflicted and what mercy dwells in every woe. Philosophy, drawing its sinews into tension and biting its lips, counts it a feat to bear trouble without a groan. But Faith, placing beneath us the arms of Everlasting Love, teaches us to cry out from the depths, "THOU hast been a strength to the poor, a strength to the needy in his distress, a refuge from the storm, a shadow from the heat, when the blast of the terrible ones is as a storm against the wall."

Taught in the school of faith, we learn that no affliction befalls us without good reason on God's part and designs of blessedness toward ourselves. Every sorrow is an essential part of the course of discipline by which our present peace is enlarged and our future bliss perfected. The vivacity thus afforded to patience, faith and hope, together with the love of abiding the whole will of God, affords a rich experience of comfort in Christ—a calmer and sweeter repose than we could expect to obtain from a life of uniform outward prosperity.

# XVI.

## THE SERVICE OF SUFFERING.

### THIRD—CHRIST SUSTAINING AND FOREARMING.

ONE of the peculiar glories of religion is nobly illustrated in this: it is a *present* help when its supports are most needed. Hours of distressing need are before us all, and who can tell but the days of darkness will be many? This side of the veil no view of Jesus is more precious than when he comes walking on the sea in the night of our anguish. How thrills the voice which is then heard above the roar of the tempest, "Be ye of good cheer; it is I; be not afraid!" How sweet the calm when, after having taken us by the hand, before the waters overwhelmed us, he comes with us into the ship! There is a good worldly maxim which says, "A friend in need is a friend indeed." But blessed above all human power to bless is union to Christ through all the present life—life as it is and will be in all human experience. On all that experience the fearful truth is deeply engraved, that

> "Grief is rooted in our souls,
> And man grows up to mourn."

It does not follow that the Christian should become a sad contemplator of the world, who sees in it nothing but gloom, and whose heart is ever strung for mournful melodies. The earth, even in its moral wreck, is still a bright and beautiful world, redolent of sweets for those who understand their enjoyment. Still, who can hope to escape a life of trouble? Who that lives only for the comforts of earth can look upon his loveliest enjoyments without a dread feeling of insecurity for the next hour? Whose feet are not, even now, bleeding from the thorns which grow in his path?

Looking soberly at what has befallen us, and what must befall us still, we feel this fullness of value in the support of Christ, that he is a near helper in the hour of need—nearest when the necessity of his friend is deepest. There is one glaring view of the worthlessness of the world as a helper, which the wild eye of sin fails to catch, viz.: *Worldly supports fail most cruelly when their need is most direfully felt.* When the spirit of the sinner is most nearly famished, then the cup is most sure to be dashed from his lips. Let the unhappy votary of the world meet a change of fortune, let prosperity forsake him and troubles throng him, and he will learn that human reliances are most inhumanly false at the exact time when their falseness is most keenly felt. The discarded favorite of Henry VIII. experienced only what thousands before him had felt, and thousands to come will feel, when he exclaimed (or rather is made to say),

> "Oh, Cromwell! Cromwell!
> Had I but served my God with half the zeal
> I served my king, he would not, in my age,
> Have left me naked to my enemies."

But the hour of extremity is our Saviour's chosen time for bringing forth his best comforts. The richest offices of his grace are reserved for exigencies when, without its aid, the spirit would be crushed. When every other stream of comfort is dry, the river from this fountain overflows its banks. The COMFORTER comes to those whom the world has cast out and trodden down, with loaded hands and words of cheer. To the mourner who dares not look around, for all is drear, he says, "Look up!" and lo! the transport of the celestial vision makes a morning of joy after a night of weeping.

Affliction becomes a means of sanctified

happiness when it is attended by an exquisite perception of the sympathy of Christ. "In all our afflictions he was afflicted." The most delightful experiences of grace are those which afford the liveliest apprehension of nearness to the Saviour. Communion with our unseen Lord is felt in almost sensual reality when he speaks to our stricken hearts of his own fellow-feeling in our grief. We are sometimes almost in wonder whether it is not a real vision to the eye of sense: we involuntarily look around, as if expecting to behold the actual "form of the fourth, like the Son of God," walking by our side in the furnace of fire, when the voice is so near and comes in such a stilling whisper: "When thou passest through the waters, I will be with thee, and through the rivers, they shall not overflow thee; when thou walkest through the fire, thou shalt not be burned, neither shall the flame kindle upon thee."

During the persecution of Christians under the Emperor Julian, one Theodorus was laid upon the rack. His executioners loosened the instrument before the fatal extreme, and gave him a brief respite, in hope that the dread of further torture would move him to renounce Christ. But he exhibited a patience so surprising that he was asked how it was possible for him to endure so much with so little demonstration of anguish. "At first," said he, "I felt pain, but afterward there appeared to stand by me a young man, who wiped the sweat from my face and frequently refreshed me with cold water, which so delighted me that I almost regretted being taken from the rack." Shall we call this vision the delusion of a fancy bewildered by the condition of the body? Not if we believe the spirit and power of the promise, "Lo! I am with you."

The bare thought of the *presence* of

Christ with us in our sorrows falls far short of what is implied in his fellow-feeling. We have no sufficient view of his supporting love until we think of him as *taking part* in our sufferings. He who draws near to sorrowing humanity with words of kindness and hope was himself the "man of sorrows." Cast off by those for whose good he came to labor and die; poorer in worldly wealth than the foxes and birds; at one time shunning a murderous mob; at another weeping tears of affliction at the grave of a dear friend, and again shrinking with human dread from the prospect of coming woes,—his catalogue of griefs seemed to embrace almost the entire sweep of mortal exposures.

His atoning death is not here brought into the account. Those were the sorrows of his life. That was the experience which arms his sympathy with such sustaining strength for us. Through his own knowledge of the conflict he is able to succor the tempted. Our griefs are written with the pen of experience upon his heart. This is the companionship of the Angel of his Presence, walking hand in hand with us through every dark way in our pilgrimage, himself plucking the thorns from our flesh, and cheering us when ready to faint by telling how he overcame and sat down with the Father in his throne, and how we shall share in the same regal triumph when we overcome.

The sorrows of life bring yet another consolation to those who are "exercised thereby." They deaden our unlawful ambitions, subdue our perversities and teach us to live more for heaven than for the world. They bring us face to face with those subjects of thought which enlarge our admiration of the government of God, and thus they increase our holiness and exalt our joys. Under the administration of that government all particular dispensations are woven into one comprehensive system of good and glory. Faith beholds in each of our trials a contribution toward the great purpose which must be consummated. By fastening our attention to these views, God leads our wills kindly along to submission to his general purpose. Self is lost in God.

*Self lost in God!* When this result is reached, his glory and our peace are inseparable. The last occasion for revolt from personal distress is removed. Our happiness is loosened from its anchorage to the selfish ground of personal prosperity, and finds its moorings in the will of God. Holding fast there, we are above trouble. All our wishes concerning providential events come around to the one desire that God should reign. He will reign for ever; and embarking our whole happiness in that truth, we shall be serene for ever. We may be forsaken, maligned, poor, disappointed in our personal ambition, broken in health, or robbed by unfeeling death of our dearest friends; but what then? These are the acts of the Divine administration, which we love better than we loved any lost good. It is "our Father at the helm," amid the fury of the winds and the surges of the ocean. God reigns, and what more do we want?

Many of our allotments may be so dark that faith itself shrinks from the inquiry why these things are so. But even then, commensurate with the mystery of the dispensation will be the peacefulness of trusting our Saviour's word, "What I do thou knowest not now, but thou shalt know hereafter." As a schooling for the endowments of heaven, trust is often better than knowledge. We are often better and happier for the necessity which resolves our carnal anxiety to know all into this sentiment of unbounded confidence: "Even so, Father, for so it seemed good in thy sight."

In holy trust there is one feature of sterling value which distinguishes the genuine from the false. The true is, throughout all the Christian's experience, an ever-living sentiment—the prevalent tone of his feelings toward the government of God. It is not a temporary exercise, produced to meet some particular trial, enduring as long as the memory of the occasion lasts, and then laid to sleep until some new affliction summons it to reawaken. True submission surveys the whole field of God's dispensation toward ourselves; it looks at his past dealings which are known, and then at the unknown future; it contemplates the vicissitudes to which we are yet exposed, as well as those which have been experienced, and acquiescing alike in all, it becomes an abiding happy confidence that our heavenly Father not only hath done, but will yet do, all things well. No reconciliation of any narrower scope has power to bring forth pure peace. This alone is the art of deriving happiness from suffering the will of God.

Submission to afflictions only at the times when they are felt is seldom anything better than the sullen patience of the philosopher, who says that since the calamity has occurred, and is beyond remedy, it may as well be peaceably endured. But a holy acquiescence in any past dealing of God leads to a similar trust in all which he is yet to do with us. We then contemplate the most precious earthly comfort which still abides with us; we think of all the happiness which it has afforded, and of what we are still expecting from the enjoyment of it; and then, without one rebellious emotion, we submit that living comfort to the dispensation of Heaven, to be left or taken—"Not as I will, but as THOU wilt." Thus accepting all dispensations to come in the same unrepining spirit which we feel toward past heavenly chastisements, we gain satisfying assurance that our resignation is the fruit of cordial attachment to the government of God.

The power of the Divine Spirit must be invoked to work in the heart this abiding satisfaction with the whole will of God. But when it is once wrought, we are armed in advance for any possible trouble. Things to come as well as things present, "all are yours." We are alike supported now and girded for all future fights with affliction. When the hour of calamity comes, the great battle with our wilful tempers is not to be fought. The question of pleasant submission is already settled, and by that early settlement of matters between ourselves and the Divine administration we have deprived tribulation of its power over our peace.

In such a frame we are sure of the support of Heaven in all our trials. Our hearts are open to the whole consolation which Christ brings to those who drink his cup and receive his baptism of sorrow. As the attractions of earth are loosened, those of heaven fasten themselves more firmly upon us. The "exceeding and eternal weight of glory" is a more beatific contemplation when it is placed in contrast with "our light affliction, which is but for a moment." Looking up from the vales of gloom, faith gains its best view of the light and glory which settles around the everlasting hills. Turning disappointed from the waters of Marah, which only mocked our thirst, how sweet to drink from the river of God!

Exemption from the sorrows of life we no longer expect until we reach the immortal shore. The enjoyment of undisturbed worldly bliss was no part of the terms under which we were admitted to discipleship. In the deed of the surrender of ourselves to Christ we left those lines which should describe our earthly portion a blank for him to fill, and we expected that many words of sorrow would be traced there. It is enough for us to know that all our corrections are with judgment, and not in anger, and that they are appointed by that Infinite Love who knows our frame and remembers that we are dust. The promise of support is confirmed by all our experience of the past and by the history of the friends of God in every age. From the darkest of his ways the brightest illustrations of his love have always shone. In all his dealings with his friends, bringing power to the faint, courage to the trembling and joy to the sorrowing, he affords us the assurance of the same grace in the same hour of need. The unbroken line of godly experience has strengthened the promise of ages gone, that "when the poor and needy seek water, and there is none, and their tongue faileth for thirst, I the Lord will hear them; I the God of Israel will not forsake them."

# XVII.

## THE BORDER LAND.

### FIRST—REASSURANCE.

IN the peace which Jesus sheds upon the living pilgrim's path we have seen his "beauty why we should desire him." We have found in his consolations this wondrous adaptation, distinguishing them from all helps which this world offers, that they are nearest at hand when other supports are most treacherous. Thus we have learned to characterize them as "grace to help in time of need."

Then can we so enthrone faith as to trust our Redeemer to the last? An event is approaching which to us is untried—a scene whose terrors for the human nature are unprecedented in all our past experience of the glooms of life. Will it not contain too many elements of dismay to allow us to maintain our serenity, even at the command of the Prince of Peace? These are becoming inquiries for the thoughtful soul, conscious of drawing near the line which divides this from the world of spirits. Will the grace which has sustained us in the trials of life be an adequate support in the darker hour of death? If we have sometimes been wearied in the race with the footmen, how will we contend with the horses? If frequently appalled in the land of peace, how will we do in the swellings of Jordan?

Let the past speak. Has God ever failed to honor the faith of his friends? In every earthly vicissitude has not the experience of his grace been such as to inspire unbounded trust for the untried future? The supports which have thus far sustained our rugged pilgrimage, have they not so illustrated the Divine method of strength for the day that we involuntarily expect something better than all the past to close up our earthly experience of the comforts of Christ? The manner in which he has drawn most near when without him we should have been most desolate, does it not arm us with confidence that, in the final conflict, the everlasting supports will be firm and gentle beyond all we have hitherto felt?

The soul listens for what God will himself speak. Inspired by the experience of the past, it expects to hear the best words of love for the darkest hour of nature. It turns to the recorded promises, and lo! it is all written, just as might have been expected, for the friend of Jesus trembling on the shore of mortality: "Yea, though I walk through the valley of the shadow of death, I will fear no evil, for thou art with me; thy rod and thy staff, they comfort me;" "We know that if our earthly house of this tabernacle were dissolved, we have a building of God, an house not made with hands, eternal in the heavens;" "My flesh and my heart faileth, but God is the strength of my heart, and my portion for ever."

We note the experience of those who have tested the sustaining power of grace to the end, and there again it is told as we should expect. "How now about that trust in the Lord, of which we have so often spoken?" was once inquired of an aged disciple on her dying bed. "Eighty years long," she replied, "my heavenly Father has borne me through every trial, and I am not afraid to trust him now." In the same community an old man rose in a public religious assembly, and said that for almost fifty years he had been striving to serve his Redeemer, and the comforts of the service had grown better and better all the time. The next week he was unexpectedly prostrated by disease, and informed that he must die. He was reminded of his words just quoted, and asked what he thought of those comforts now. "Still better and better," he replied; "Christ is all my support, but he is enough. I can truly say my cup runneth over." Numerous examples of this highest power of sustaining grace in the utmost extremity confirm the trembling believer's faith. If we can but yield our souls to its influence, the bitterness of death is already past. We lose our dread of contemplating

> "The scene where Christians die—
> Whêre holy souls retire to rest."

"The "trembling" and "lingering" notes drop out from the song, while the "hoping," "flying," and "bliss of dying," swell more joyous from the valley, the bank and the midst of the river, until they are absorbed in the celestial harmonies which sweep from the harps of gold.

We do not however look for uniformity in the manifestations of this one spirit of overcoming faith. The type of Christian emotion varies in different minds during life; and there is no magic in a dying bed to reduce all constitutional tempers to one cast. Different minds will experience differing operations of the faith which Jesus reserves for the dying hour of his friends, ranging from tranquillity to ecstasy, and there will be a similar variety in the outward expression of this faith.

One is triumphant in death. The conqueror's sword is in his hand, and the victor's shout on his lips. Leaning on Christ, he defies the powers of darkness. He is on the wing, and his spirit is already as tuneful as a seraph's. He is straitened for words to publish his joy, and he would gladly summon the universe to come and hear what God is doing for him.

Another carries a feeling of self-abasement to the last. The thought that he is just about to be for ever saved by grace arrays all his personal unworthiness once more before his view, and he only dares to say that, as an undeserving sinner, he dies trusting in Christ.

The feelings of another are placid and his expressions are calm. His soul melts under a view of the great mercy of God. He has long been accustomed to obtain from the quiet visits of his Saviour's love more comfort than he has told of, and the present aspects of his experience are deep and gentle peace. There is little that is apparent to distinguish this hour from other seasons of life. He served God while living, and built his hope gradually but firmly on the cross of Christ. The great change through which he is passing is an event long familiar to his meditations. His work is done, and what remains for him in this world but to die?

These are the "diversities of operations" of "the same Spirit," and "it is the same God which worketh all in all." Under all these exhibitions of confidence, wherever we see evidence of their genuineness, we recognize the repose of the soul under the shadow of dying faith. Christ is the rod and staff, comforting them all along their march through the valley of the shadow of death. The one voice which they all speak is, "What time I am afraid, I will trust in thee."

The range from within which thoughts tributary to this peace may be gathered up is wide. The glory to be revealed breaks upon the eye on which the world is darkening in a rich variety of lights. There are exemptions and acquisitions, excellent losses and no less excellent gains, beauties of character and beatitudes of state, all embraced in that which is the best and the pledge of them all—the covenant of everlasting love. These are the things which are hung like lamps of heaven all around the valley of the shadow of death.

Among the elements of this peace, deliverance from the anguish of the sinner's last hours holds no mean place. There is no light in the dying chamber where pardon has not been spoken and hope does not come. Death, viewed simply as an event in the course of nature, is fearful enough to all. But with the soul whose departure is hopeless of mercy all its natural solemnness is absorbed in the frightful expectation of meeting the Judge and hearing the final doom. Then thoughts of unforgiven sin crowd upon the conscience, and the frowns of an angry God come in vision before the dying sinner's eye. It would seem sufficiently dreadful to be forced to a sullen, reluctant and eternal parting from a world where all his affections are treasured, and beyond which he has not a single object of love. But even the thought of what he is leaving is often forgotten in the wilder thought of whither he is going. The helpless debtor who has allowed an account to roll up against himself until he is afraid even to think how large it must be, looks appalled upon the summons to a reckoning. So with the poor soul out of Christ and on the last inch of time; he has nothing but liabilities on the book of heaven, and now the day of settlement has come. The long disagreement between himself and God is henceforth past reconciliation. For him the door of mercy, which is now closing, will open no more.

But sad as this contemplation is, what glory it lends to the contrast! Justified in the atonement and secured by the intercession of the Redeemer, the believer dies under his Lord's reconciling grace. He is removed from the world in love, not in wrath. He knows that his Redeemer liveth, and he expects to stand under the shelter of his advocacy when he appears before God. Sins, from the curse of which he has already obtained redemption, are not allowed to flit around his pillow and frighten him with dismal apprehensions. Death has not come to change him from one state of sinfulness to a lower depth of depravity, nor to remove him from a world of hope to a realm of despair. All through his past pilgrim days the voice which first told him to be of good cheer, for his sins were forgiven, has remained in his soul like the lingering vibrations of some song of the skies. Now its echoes are filling, and they more than renew the transports which they first awoke. Where has language any terms for expressing the beauty of such a thought as this—he dies justified, adopted and sanctified, in peace with God! He is sustained by that which is even better than hope, for his Lord is there. It is the voice of the Messenger of the Covenant which says, "I am with you." He listens and knows THE PRESENCE in his soul.

# XVIII.

## THE BORDER LAND.

### SECOND—THE GLOOM AND THE LIGHT.

THE awfulness of death, viewed only as a natural occurrence, has been mentioned. Let us retouch those sombre shades, that they may give vividness to the contrast when the covenant of Christ is exhibited as a sanctuary from the carnal dread of dying.

Independent of all moral considerations, gloom gathers around the subject of death. It is regarded as the crowning calamity of human existence—that which men take most care to avoid and expect with most dread. "All that a man hath will he give for his life." As a figure, death is often employed to afford the most terrible impression of objects. When we say of any allotment, that it is bitter as death, or of any human passion, that it is cruel as the grave, we mean to make the darkest representation of it which words will afford.

These gloomy views of death approach every mind. The friends of Christ are often slow in rising above them. They are not strictly afraid to die; that is, they have no tormenting dread of the event. They expect their Redeemer to be with them, and they look for peace from his presence. But the involuntary recoil of nature often lingers, like the muscular tremblings of a healed patient, not as the sign of present disease, but the token of its past severity. We "start at death's alarms," and we should probably be agitated by the unexpected intelligence that we have not another day to live.

Among these natural glooms of death faith does its reassuring work as truly as when dealing with its moral terrors. Trust in the covenant is the sanctuary whose portals shut the Christian in and the dreads without.

One of the dark aspects of death, when viewed from the stand-point of human nature, is *the separation of the dying from all that is dear to them on earth.* Things and friends who have been objects of familiarity and fondness are now to be lost in the darkness of earth. We leave them all; mere earthly love is no more. The parting scene is solemn and affecting. It is an hour when the natural affections are awakened to the most excessive tenderness of which they are susceptible; and the one who is passing away often shares their intensity with those who are weeping around his bed. The sorrow of sundering natural ties is inseparable from natural love, and there is nothing derogatory to the character of piety in a falling tear and parting pang, which betray that something is sacrificed for the final gain of everything. God never intended that holy affections should make us cold to the natural attachments of life. Our Lord and Master, Jesus himself, wept true human tears at the grave of his friend. Far from us be that religion which would turn our humanity into stone!

But the past experiences of grace have all along prepared the dying Christian for these painful separations. The objects of his holy affections have gradually multiplied, and he has been inspired with a growing love for the employments, the company, the Saviour and the King of heaven, until it has become with him a settled state of feeling that, good as it might seem to remain for the comfort of friends, it will be infinitely better to depart and be with Christ. God has wrought within him the habit of keeping a loose hold of present delights, and taught him to live more upon such abiding joys as he can carry with him, than upon the pleasures which can go no farther than earth. In such ways he has forearmed his friends against any overwhelming sorrow, when the hour of parting comes. They lose only what they expected to leave when the soul should stretch her wings for her passage to the skies. What was really unworthy of their love they have learned to disregard. What was worthy of their attachment, but was only adapted to their comfort as passing travelers, is easily exchanged for the superior delights of their abiding home.

The friend of God, feeling that his eyes are about to close upon the world for ever, may ask to be carried to the window of his chamber. There he may look out for the last time upon the rising sun, the glowing sky, the green wood and sprightly brook where he has had so many pleasant rambles, and the arbor around which his own hands taught the vine to entwine itself in so tasteful beauty. What if a shadow does cross his brow, at the thought that he is to look upon these delightful things of God no more? It is but a shadow, and that for a moment only, for the eternal sun is rising, and faith even now is gazing upon skies which are never darkened. He forsakes the strolls of earth to walk along the river clear as crystal, shaded by the tree of life. There can be no disturbing sorrow in the change, when the same breath which bids the world farewell welcomes heaven.

So much of the affection between the dying believer and the friends from whom he parts as has been sanctified by their mutual love of Christ, will remain unbroken. Love which has been refined by grace is immortal. There is no reason to suppose that death ever suspends the attachment of the glorified spirit for the pious friends whom he has left in the world.

The Christian reader can now fix his thoughts upon some former companions of his pilgrimage who have outstripped him in the heavenly race, and are at home with Christ. They were dear—God only knows how dear!—while you walked together below. Their love for you was never warmer and purer than at the moment when they rejoiced to leave your immediate society for that of heaven. You know their departure has not changed your affection for them, and can you suppose it has weaned them from you? Subordinate to the place which God occupies, the bereaved Christian has in his heart a little altar where his glorified friend is enshrined; and the fire of that altar is fanned by the breath of many prayers for a blessed reunion where those who meet part no more. And why should we suppose that any holy fondness has been extinguished in the hearts of those who are now among the spirits of the just, because they have exchanged this chilly abode for that world where,

> "Kept by a Father's hand,
> Love cannot die?"

God's word makes it certain that heaven is a scene of the holiest and happiest social attachments. All the fondness which on earth was really worthy of nourishment is there preserved and purified; and there the range of affections is enlarged by the soul's coming into intimacy with new and nobler objects of regard.

With such visions opening, the parting trials at death lose their power over the peace of the dying Christian. The view of faith brightens in proportion as the film gathers over the outward eye. We shall see less and less of what we are leaving, while we have enlarging views of the compensating gains. What were the losses of earth to the Christian martyrs who, "full of the Holy Ghost, looked up steadfastly into heaven, and saw the glory of God and Jesus standing on the right hand of God." "Farewell," said a noble Roman of the Imperial age, departing from the world—"farewell, oh farewell, all earthly things! and welcome heaven! From this time let none speak of earthly things to me!" For one who in this spirit is plumed for the upward flight, what are the pangs of departing farewells?

While the Christian is in the border land, faith comes to his aid against another of the natural glooms of death—*the dread of the unknown beyond.*

Into this darkness Divine grace alone can shine. Philosophy has no light to penetrate it. The wisdom of man has neither explored that mysterious thing which we call death, nor looked with any rational views upon its probable issues beyond our present sight. To one who rejects the knowledge which God has imparted on the subject, it always appears as it did to the unbeliever, Hobbes, who in his last moments said, with horror, "I am taking a fearful leap in the dark!"

In the mind of Columbus and his intrepid fellow-mariners, embarking for the search of a western world, there must have been a solemn excitement in the thought that they were spreading their sails for unknown seas, from whence no voyager had returned with tidings. Still, in their case, the excitement of hope prevailed over that of dread. They hoped, at some distant day, to revisit the land and friends from whom they parted, and to astound Europe with tidings from a hitherto undiscovered realm of the globe.

But no gallant ship returns to the shores of *Time*. Millions have sailed away, millions more are now casting off from their earthly moorings; but not one has returned. No human gaze follows their track, to see what seas they ride or beneath what billows they sink—what worlds they reach or what eternal wanderings they pursue. The gloom of contemplating this voyage is oppressive.

The mystery of death is itself terrible. That thing *death*—what does it mean? What is it to die? What makes the distinction between the living and the lifeless state? What is that peculiar sensation which men call the pang of parting life? There are none to tell us; the lips from which alone we could learn are all mute.

But there is a still deeper dread of the unexplored mysteries beyond. Those who reject the lights and supports of the gospel of Christ often feel their souls tossed widely by the alternations of desire and repulsion—a strange conflict between longing to know and shrinking from learning. In a quiet country cemetery in one of our old States, lie the remains of two men, neighbors in life, and both of them professed disbelievers in Divine revelation. While they were both alive they entered into the strange covenant that the one who first left the world should, if he found any future state of being, return if possible and inform the other respecting it. One died and was buried. The survivor, as long as he lived, avoided passing that graveyard in the dark. To his dying day he shrank affrighted at the thought of the bargained visit from the world of spirits. Well, those men know it all now. But on this side of the boundary all to human sense is as dark as ever.

While, under the other mortal terrors, the *love of Christ* is the all-sufficient support, this gloom is effectually dispersed by the *Light of God.* Faith sits down in the school of Divine inspiration. There, under the teachings of Heaven, that which was mystery becomes the best of all knowledge—revealed truth. Ignorance of the nature of death, or of the destiny which it opens, then ceases to be an element of the dread of dying. Faith inspires the believer with such assurance of the word of God that he adopts whatever the Holy Spirit teaches as *known truth.* Enlightened by this "evidence of things not seen," he rests from his dread of the unknown, for with this light in his soul what unknown is there to dread? He asks, What is it to die? and the answer is brought by that "earnest of the Spirit" by which Paul was taught, when he described it as simply the dissolving of this earthly house of our tabernacle. *We* do not die. That which has been well termed the mud-walled cottage in which we live, goes to ruin under the law of nature which assigns to all physical structures the periods of growth, maturity and decline. *We* are immortal.

The Christian again asks respecting what lies beyond. The same "earnest of the Spirit" speaks to him of the home provided for *himself* when the earthly tabernacle is dissolved—"We have a building of God, an house not made with hands, eternal in the heavens." He is not to be "unclothed, but clothed upon, that mortality might be swallowed up of life." From the lips of Christ a like view of what awaits his dying friends is conveyed under the same pleasant figure of a house—an immortal home: "In my Father's house are many mansions; if it were not so, I would have told you: I go to prepare a place for you. And if I go to prepare a place for you, I will come again and receive you unto myself, that where I am there ye may be also."

For the soul thus illuminated no painful obscurity clouds the subject of death. The satisfied heart looks across all the intervening space to the "building of God," the house and home where Christ is and we shall be also; and with so much in view that is clear, it is willing to rest from further explorings until called to pursue them in worlds of light.

Much reason, it is true, remains for saying, "It doth not yet appear what we shall be;" still the departing saint feels all his solicitude calmed while he does "know that when HE shall appear, we shall be like him, for we shall see him as he is." He knows enough to assure him that he will enjoy unspeakable gain in the change from the mortal to the immortal state. He knows also that this transition is an object of the complacency of his heavenly Father, for again the Spirit says, "Precious in the sight of the Lord is the death of his saints." Thus fleeing to the sanctuary of Christian faith, he finds sweet repose from the fearful thought of launching out on unknown seas or wandering in "undiscovered bourns."

# XIX.

## THE BORDER LAND.

### THIRD—THE COVENANT SLUMBER.

THERE remains for notice one more of the natural terrors of death—*the gloom of the grave.*

It is a cold, dark abode, where corruption is our father and the worm our mother and sister. There is a universal shrinking of human nature from this destiny. Here we rejoice in the light and warmth of heaven, but there all is cold night upon which our sun never rises. We delight in the social communings of earth, but there we shall lie alone. No cheering word of friendship enters the "dull, cold ear of death." The most endeared earthly friends may be buried in the same coffin, still the dead are all alone. The sepulchre can never become social.

> "Silence and solitude and gloom
> In those forgetful realms appear."

Physical systems which are now rich in the strength and activity of life must there lie in long paralysis. Forms which are now beautiful will become a sightless mass of corruption, which the grave in mercy hides from the eye of the living.

Is Christian faith an overmatch for the dread which the carnal sense feels at the approach of such a doom? Yes, and more: it brings out from this very doom the highest personal triumph which the cross gives to the believer. Here, perhaps more than anywhere else, religion is true to its own nature—that is, most available at the time of greatest need. The gospel writes its richest words upon the walls of the tomb. Its crowning conquest is victory over the grave.

The heart of the thoughtful friend of Christ has often lingered lovingly over the phrase, *sleeping in Jesus*—"Them also which sleep in Jesus will God bring with him." In this figure there is something which speaks the practical sympathy of Christ in the darkest of our allotments. Let this be marked well: it is a sympathy which is felt not alone in the cold passage over the river, but one that still abides with the flesh which the life has deserted. In the language of our creed, "He was crucified, dead and *buried*." In taking his part in all our trials, he

"Passed through the grave, and blessed the bed."

But even this does not reach the true idea of *sleeping in Jesus*. Nothing short of an evangelical view of the provisions of the eternal covenant of redemption will disclose the blessedness which dwells in those touchingly simple words. Christ with his own blood *purchased* his redeemed ones. The Father, under covenant promise, gave them to him as the *reward* of his expiatory death. Their *perfect redemption from all the dominion of sin* is to become the highest power of his cross and the basis of his greatest mediatorial glory. Nothing of the *redeemed* man, nothing of the Redeemer's *purchased possession*, must remain an eternal monument of the power of sin and death.

Here the glorious truth of the RESURRECTION bursts upon the vision of faith. The voice of promise and summons to the Church is heard from the Lord of the purchased bodies and souls of his people: "Thy dead men shall live; together with my dead body shall they arise: awake and sing, ye that dwell in dust! for thy dew is as the dew of herbs, and the earth shall cast out the dead."

Here the Redeemer's interest in the dying body is found to be the same as in the undying soul. They are alike parts of his covenant property. He received no fractional part of the believer's nature, but that believer is given to him as a whole man, and in that whole Jesus is to be admired in the final triumphal glory of his cross. He has then the same cause for a jealous care of the body as for the soul. To himself, as well as to the unworthy subject of his grace, the protection and final glorifying of the whole man is an object of inexpressible interest. The same omniscient love which, during the intermediate state, guards the disembodied spirit, will keep its post of vigil where the flesh is reposing beyond the reach of weariness and sin. In the grave, or down in the coral chambers of the ocean, or unburied on some desert wild, this flesh may moulder until every vestige of human form shall disappear: still it remains an essential covenant possession of Christ, which he has perfect power and perfect purpose to keep. It sleeps in the covenant, and that is sleeping in Jesus.

What mournings the corruption of the outward nature is ever bringing upon the children of God! What wrestlings of spirit with these bodies, the mediums of depraved inclination and instruments of sin! How the Christian has longed for the wings of a dove, that he might fly away and be at rest! Brought forth from the grave, all this will be to him "the former things which are passed away." Then the Redeemer is to present his people unblemished—"a glorious Church, not having spot or wrinkle, or any such thing." The grave is to be made to the body the instrument of purification, removing its grossness and preparing it for the reunion with the spirit—a restored being with angelic attainments.

Expecting this refining process through death and the grave, should we any longer shrink from abandoning this flesh to corruption? At present we trace many of our sins and sorrows to its wants and its yearnings for evil. God forbid that we should ever carry such earthly wants and corrupt tendencies to heaven! The grave will hide them for ever, while the "Watcher and Holy One" brings forth, in his own time, the pure form like his own risen body. How sublime the description from the pen of the writer to the Corinthians—from corruption to incorruption, from dishonor to glory, from weakness to power, from an animal to a spiritual body! Spirit of God! inspire us also with the assured hope of such a resurrection, and we will cease to look into the grave as a dark dungeon where the tyrant Sin holds his sullen ward. With Paul we will stand over the tomb and extol the triumph of grace: "O Death! where is thy sting? O Grave! where is thy victory?"

In the heart of one who has been the

subject of an earnest Christian experience this hope is too well inwrought to be disturbed by the cavils of human wisdom. The comforts of the doctrine of the resurrection were not first suggested by the science of this world, and they are not to be darkened by the philosophy of men. The truth belongs entirely to another department of knowledge—the revealed wisdom of God. Vain sophists may array their physiological theories against our hopes; they may talk about the same atoms changing from body to body; they may palter about the question whether the preservation of the particles of matter in the human system is essential to the identity of the body itself; they may go farther and commit blasphemy by denying the power of God to reproduce forms after the utter ruin of organic structure, so that the thing formed shall be, not another being, but the same man who once before lived: it is enough for us that, as we first accepted these hopes from God, we rely upon his truth and power to accomplish what he has said.

More than this, we throw into the face of skeptical philosophy its own voidness of reason when it perpetrates the absurdity of bringing mere human science to sit in judgment upon truths which belong only to the Infinite Mind. It is blind to one of the most obvious distinctions in sound reasoning, when it can see no difference between *contrary to reason and above reason*, and so sets down everything which is beyond its own grasp as unphilosophical.

When we do see that with the same ashy dust, acted upon alike by the second causes of moisture, warmth, and light, God disposes some particles into the form and tint of the rose, others into the modest violet or gorgeous magnolia, and still others into the golden fruits of summer, giving to each of these such a body as pleases himself, we find no difficulty in believing his power to work his own pleasure with the mouldered remains of the human form. In neither case do we understand the process. But in one instance we witness the result, and the result is all that concerns us in the other. The truth of his covenant is the point that is settled in our hearts, and reposing in the trust that we shall awake in the likeness of Christ, the grave is gloomy no longer.

> "On the cold cheek of death smiles and roses are blending,
> And beauty immortal awakes from the tomb."

*In our flesh* we shall see God. *Our eyes*, and not those of another shall behold him.

These, together with those suggested in preceding articles, are the supports under which the friend of Christ dies. The moral terrors of death are overcome by forgiving grace and justifying faith. Its natural glooms have undergone the alchemy of the cross, transmuting each thing of dread into an element of triumph. All is then clear. The Christian's departure is not alone an occasion for pious submission: it should be an event of real joy.

So it has been felt by men of God, inspired and uninspired. Look at Paul: "To me, to live is Christ, and to die is gain;" "Death is swallowed up in victory;" "Willing rather to be absent from the body, and to be present with the Lord." Such experiences of holy men abound on the records of the Divine Word. The Psalmist of Israel has before been quoted: "Though I walk through the valley of the shadow of death, I will fear no evil, for thou art with me; thy rod and thy staff, they comfort me." Many of that day went up in spirit, as Elijah did visibly, amid the parting skies, in a chariot of fire. And so they have done since, and will continue to do, until "thy people pass over, O Lord! till the people pass over which thou hast purchased."

From the ranks of the learned and the unlearned, the lowly and the illustrious, examples almost without limit come forth to strengthen our trust. Here is the poor mutilated English sailor, of whom Dr. Griffin, of Portsea, wrote. "Come in," said he, as his minister entered the room, "come in, thou man of God! I have been longing to tell you the happy state of my mind. I shall soon die, but death has now no terrors. I am going to heaven. Oh what has Jesus done for me, one of the vilest of the human race! The joy I feel from the sense of the love of God to sinners, and the thought of being with the Saviour, are more than I can express. Hallelujah! hallelujah!"

We go to the dying bed of Dr. Finley, former President of the College of New Jersey. "I know not," said he, "in what language to speak of my own unworthiness. I have been undutiful. . . . I can truly say that I have loved the service of God. I have honestly endeavored to act for God, but with much weakness and corruption. . . . Oh that each of you may experience what, blessed be God, I do, when you come to die! . . . Eternal rest is at hand; the Lord hath given me victory; I exult! I triumph!"

Most of the readers of Christian biography are familiar with the dying experience of that young servant of Christ, James Brainerd Taylor. "Heaven," he said, "never appeared more desirable. I have longed to see the King in his beauty. Never did I gain so near an access to God. Dying seems like going to my Father's house. . . . I have longed, *longed*, to enter heaven. . . . My active spirit, which now clings to Jesus, will be adoring, active, and wondering among the spirits of the just made perfect. . . .

It is but a little way from this to yonder mansion. . . . How sweet the earnest! Only a little while, and we shall be there."

Room for examples fails. From such dying chambers visions of glory blaze. As we gaze on them, we seem to go up "from the plains of Moab unto the mountain of Nebo, to the top of Pisgah," and look out upon the scene beyond. We cannot more appropriately close our contemplations of this side of the river than here in sight of Canaan.

# XX.

## HEAVEN.

### FIRST—THINGS WHICH EYE HATH NOT SEEN NOR EAR HEARD.

THE astronomer, attempting to explore remote worlds, is obliged to take his standpoint of observation on this earth. He cannot carry his instruments into the field of discovery, and there measure celestial magnitudes or bring to light the wonders of those distant creations. What he observes by looking across the long interval must suffice, for he can learn no more.

Thus, for a little while, we are circumscribed in our views of heaven. It is a distant land, which the foot of none living on earth has trodden. Its scenes are without the range of sense, and its glory surpasses the power of human comprehension. Here we can neither survey it with the eyes of glorified spirits nor speak of it in the language of the skies. One who enjoyed a supernatural view of that world gave only this shorn account of his beatific vision, that there he "heard unspeakable words which it is not lawful [possible] for a man to utter." We are indebted to our faith for so much account as God has sent across from thence to this dim-sighted world, for all our heavenly discoveries this side of death.

And these discoveries are sufficient now. Even through this dark glass men have seen what has filled them with as much rapture as a mortal man knows how to bear. The last words of John Welch, one of the champions of Scotch Protestantism, uttered under overpowering manifestations of the Divine glory, were, "It is enough, O Lord—it is now enough! Hold thy hand! Thy servant is a clay vessel, and can hold no more." As much of peace and joy as our present natures can receive from the contemplation of that world is now within our reach. Like the group sketched by the sanctified fancy of Bunyan, we may now stand on the Delectable Mountains, and through the glass of faith look over to the Celestial City for which we are girded pilgrims, and where our pilgrimage will soon end. It does not impair the bliss of our anticipations to reflect that "it doth not yet appear what we shall be," for we shall know all when our souls are great enough to enjoy all.

In what lovely imagery the Divine revelation has clothed heavenly realities, so as to bring them as near as possible to our weak senses! The things which God hath prepared for them that love him, have never found a human language in which their living majesty can be written. This may be the reason why the Holy Spirit, in describing them, has so often used those pictured terms which, through our quick sense of external beauties, find their way to our hearts.

Thus the holy city, the New Jerusalem, is represented "coming down from God out of heaven, prepared as a bride adorned for her husband." The original paradise of our first parents fills all our ideas of outward pleasantness and exquisite natural enjoyments. The Spirit seizes upon this glowing ideal when it represents heaven as the "Paradise of God." It is also the "Tabernacle of God with men." There is "the Fountain of the Water of Life," and the feast which is there spread is "the Marriage Supper of the Lamb." In those regions there are no alternations of day and night, no rising and setting sun or feebler lights of evening. "The glory of God did lighten it, and the Lamb is the light thereof." Exhibited under the figure of a city walled with jasper, built of pure gold like unto glass, its foundations garnished with all manner of precious stones, the view of heaven fills all our conceptions of gorgeousness and outward loveliness. It seems as though the Spirit of inspiration had exhausted the splendors of the natural world in searching out emblems of the glory of the "city which hath foundations, whose Builder and Maker is God."

But the Holy Scriptures have plain writings, as well as charming pictures, of the scenes of everlasting rest. The Divine word affords many more descriptions of the glory to be revealed, and we repose upon promises which we believe will have a literal fulfillment. If we dwell in the golden city or walk the bank of the crystal river only in a figure, we shall literally be with Christ where he is. If we are not strictly arrayed in white robes, we shall truly possess the purity of which they are the emblems. Shining figures of speech can here promote no extravagant views. There is enough literal description to show that they are as far short of the reality as terrestrial things are beneath the celestial.

To the believer every thought of the world of bliss is delightful. In every condition this side of heaven the comforts of religion seem to fight their way to our souls against counteracting glooms. Earthly dispensations all have a dark as well as bright side, and the reflections which support our courage and console our hearts reach us only as, in the military sense of the word, they *overcome* the gloomy views which our condition suggests. But looking beyond the sins, toils and sorrows of life, we are out of the reach of all dark thoughts. We can never indulge one unpleasant view of heaven, or feel one shrinking revolt from the approach of its bliss. Every condition of life from which suffering is expected is left behind when we step within the veil. All that can inspire gloomy forbodings belongs to the former things which are passed away. Distant as our present point of observation is, we can nevertheless see that no clouds float in those skies and the sun of that everlasting day is never obscured.

God has not only prepared these things for those that love him, but he has also prepared *them* for this bliss. When we find ourselves capable of deriving happiness from such prospects, we recognize the forming work of the Divine Spirit on our hearts, and we know that God has wrought us for this selfsame thing. Throughout the whole range of heavenly enjoyments there is nothing to excite one yearning of the carnal mind. In the possessor of such a mind the wish to ascend to heaven when he dies is prompted only by the unwelcome certainty that he must leave this world, and his dread of a worse doom beyond the grave. Earth would be his supreme good if he might retain it. He has no heart for the songs of angels, the communion of the redeemed and the smile of God. Compared with present delights, the themes of that world are insipid, its associations dull and its employments irksome. This shows how much is implied when we speak of want of *preparation* for heaven.

But the believer's *earnest delight* in the prospect of the heaven which God describes, magnifies the inworking power of Divine grace. God has taken in hand the work of revolutionizing his heart, imparting to him such susceptibilities and aspirations as fit him not merely to reach that world, but to *enjoy* it. Turning wearily from a world of sin, he can sympathize in the sentiment which forms the last record in the diary of Henry Martyn —"Oh when shall time give place to eternity? When shall appear that new heaven and new earth wherein dwelleth righteousness? There, there shall in no wise enter in anything that defileth. None of that wickedness which has made men worse than wild beasts, none of those corruptions which add still more to the miseries of mortality, shall be seen or heard of any more." Before the soul in which the Holy Spirit has wrought such views of what is wearisome on the one hand or refreshing on the other, heaven glows as the object of sweet thoughts and burning hopes. Weary and heavy laden, it approaches that world for rest.

Yes, *for rest.* "There remaineth therefore a rest to the people of God." The calamities of life are past. Not only is a world of joy reached, but a world of sorrow is forsaken. For that region of endless life the pilgrim has exchanged a realm of death. Here we ride an ocean, always stormy and often lashed by the tempest into fury: there, we are told, there is no more sea. Here, we struggle with poverty, waste under diseases and "mourn departed friends." Common consent has named our present abode a vale of tears. The weak are oppressed, the unfortunate are forsaken, the ambitious are disappointed, and "the whole creation groaneth and travaileth in pain together until now." There, "they shall hunger no more, neither thirst any more, neither shall the sun light on them, nor any heat. For the Lamb which is in the midst of the throne shall feed them, and shall lead them unto the living fountains of waters, and God shall wipe away all tears from their eyes." Sorrow, crying, pain and death are among "the former things which are passed away." None of their inhabitants say, "I am sick;"

no gloomy funeral processions pass along the streets, for the days of their mourning are ended. "Neither can they die any more, for they are equal unto the angels, and are the children of God, being the children of the resurrection."

But these are only exemptions from natural evils. There is a better repose than even this for the weary wrestler with depravity. A world of sin is exchanged for a world of holiness. Here there is strife against inbred corruption and against wickedness all around. We are weary with the sight of human vileness on every hand, and we long also to possess for ourselves the perfect holiness of heaven. What a new world of enjoyment will be opened when we cease to witness the rage of human passions, to look on the oppressor trampling the poor in the dust, to hear the language of profanity, to see the ordinances of God treated with derision, and to behold men proud of their impiousness, glorying in their shame! What a new life when our own hearts are exalted above every selfish emotion, cleansed from all impure affections, and secured in the undisturbed possession of the love of God!

Heaven without trouble, sickness and death, would be a spiritual emptiness, were it not heaven without sin. It will be a thousand-fold reward for all the pains of death, if we may escape the presence of that which fills the world with dying groans. This terrible foe never invades the heavenly rest. "There shall in no wise enter into it anything that defileth, neither whatsoever worketh abomination or maketh a lie." "When He shall appear, we shall be like him, for we shall see him as he is." The moral character of every one around us will be conformed to the holiness of God. We shall be like them, and, with them, like Jesus, and pure as God is pure.

The thought is at once triumphant and humbling. Who are we, and what is our race, that such victory and award should await us? What an example of grace abounding over the deserts of sin! From the dust we raise our eyes to that glory. We feel that our nothingness is deep, according to the loftiness of our hope.

But let no carnal notions of *rest* gather around the truth of the everlasting *sabbatism* that remains to the people of God. We connect with it no thought of cessation of holy activities. We look also for such earnest and delightful mental employments as give to the soul loftier conceptions of the great glory of God. We know not the range of subjects of inquiry, but we expect no deadening of the ambition for knowledge and no slackening of the race of science.

In the present world every new intellectual attainment imparts pleasure. Our minds are formed for investigation. It lies in their nature to derive satisfaction from the discovery of truth in an endless variety of subjects. We wish to lay the universe under contribution to this propensity, and are impatient under any restriction of the field of inquiry. We wish to learn from the earth, the sea, the stars, the records of history, the labyrinths of lines and numbers, the wilds of metaphysics, the laws of moral government, and the principles of the throne of heaven. In short, wherever truth may be traced, we delight to search her footsteps and we triumph in every new discovery.

This thirst for knowledge is not a carnal propensity belonging to the earthly nature, and along with that nature to be shaken off in death. It is one of the signatures of the immortal nature—a divine instinct, imperishable as the soul's existence. Then who can doubt but these aspirations will be intensified when our sensual thraldom is all shaken off, and we are brought under circumstances which at once incite and reward the search for truth? No expectation is more rational than that this will be our condition in heaven. The wonders of boundless worlds will probably be open to our view. And who can tell but sciences so exalted that their faintest light never dawned upon earth may then spread themselves before the mind that is enlarged to know infinite things? And what will become of our present distinction of the mental from the moral when there is no philosophy of which God is not the heart—when he is felt in all and filling all? And will there be any partial application of the term "exact sciences" when all becomes more than mathematical certainty, every discovery clear and every demonstration infallible?

Under this flood of illumination the government of God will be vindicated from the charge of disorder. Reasons will be apparent why everything should exist as it does; why the sparrow should fall or kingdoms hasten to their dissolution; why the world should be cursed with sin or the Redeemer die to restore it from its revolt from God; why Christian lands should be enlightened, and the heathen left in darkness; why the redeemed should be glorified and the reprobate left in eternal woe. Every event will be seen to have its exact place in a perfect system. We shall rest from the weariness of human disputes, the impatience of pursuing truth under so many disadvantages, and the trial of understanding so little of the ways of God. That "HEREAFTER," when we are to know what Christ does, though we know not now, is then come. We look no more through the dark glass: we see face to face. We are done with this knowing in part: we know even as we are known.

# XXI.

## HEAVEN.

### SECOND—THE EVERLASTING SABBATH.

WE have ruled out from the Sabbath rest of heaven the sensual idea of inactivity. Whatever secures against weariness fulfills the import of the term. Gracious exercises are doubtless one in substance on earth and in heaven. Here they find their healthiness and their joy in living and doing for Christ. How can we but suppose that a mere passive reception of Divine comforts would be more felt as unnatural to the heavenly life in proportion as the soul's absorption in God is there more perfect?

Every description which we have of

the condition of the celestial company involves the idea of activity. And there is no reason to suppose this activity is restricted to a few forms of exercise. The glass through which we now look into that world is too dark to enable us to describe the routine of duty through which we are to pass, but such leading views of the subject as we are able to take indicate the opening of a vast and varied field of holy effort. God has around him there a countless throng of agents to do his will. The number of them is "ten thousand times ten thousand, and thousands of thousands." The use of the instrumentality of created agents is, so far as we know, his chosen method of prosecuting his designs. His field of operation is a universe without limit. Over the whole of this field events in endless variety are to be carried forward through eternal duration. With these facts before us, we naturally expect to see him assigning to his servants a vast extent of duties, various in kind and noble in character. In this boundless field for the improvement of every talent and the employment of every power, we look for opportunity for the exercise of the energies of all. The subject is captivating, but it approaches too near the unsafe ground of human speculation to render it proper to theorize minutely. We may, however, rely upon one conclusion: if we are Christ's, we shall soon enter upon angelic employments, and derive from our duties such joy as fills the heart of a seraph.

Only a faint uncertainty clouds the idea that the glorified spirits of the departed are now ministering to the friends of Christ on earth. This delightful work is unquestionably performed by messengers sent from the realms of bliss. God has explicitly promised that his angels shall have charge over those who make him their refuge, to keep them in all their ways. It was an angel that shut the mouths of the lions among whom his servant Daniel was thrown. Angels carried Lazarus to the bosom of Abraham; and the "little ones," whom we are warned not to despise, have angels who always behold the face of God in heaven. In short, they are "all ministering spirits, sent forth to minister to them who shall be heirs of salvation."

It is also beyond the reach of doubt that glorified spirits from this earth possess angelic properties. Some of those who have departed have certainly revisited the world, as angels are said to hold intercourse with earth.* Still, we have not sufficient light respecting the intermediate state between death and the resurrection to justify many positive conclusions respecting the present employment of the departed saints. The best of our knowledge concerning them, previous

* See among the other examples, Matt. xvii. 3.

to the restoration of their bodies, is that they are present with the Lord, and in that presence there is fullness of joy.

But their final employment in ministering to the glory of God is a point on which the Divine testimony is explicit. Whatever stations they may hold under the government of heaven, upon whatever embassies they may be sent, or whatever mutual offices of love may pass between them, it is certain they will always have something to do which will give them the happy assurance that they are glorifying their Lord and Redeemer. They will for ever rejoice in the consciousness that they are making practical returns of gratitude for the mercy which they have received. Their voices are among those of many angels round about the throne, and the living ones, and the elders, whose number was ten thousand times ten thousand and thousands of thousands, and whose song heard in the apocalyptic vision was, "Worthy is the Lamb that was slain to receive power and riches and wisdom and strength and honor and glory and blessing!" Their public presence in the final judgment will yield its revenue of honor to Christ, for he is then to be admired in all them that believe; and they will be for ever "a crown of glory in the hand of the Lord, and a royal diadem in the hand of God."

Even in this world, life without some great worthy end is a scene of discontent, a bubble, a farce. Existence which is not expended on some sufficient object drags wearily along. So it would doubtless be in heaven, and as much more so as the powers of activity are more quickened in the atmosphere of the world of life. Living and doing for God here ennobles and intensifies life. Then how it exalts our anticipations of that world, which is *all life*, to think of it as still living and doing for God!

Lifting our thoughts to another reach of celestial meditations, we find ourselves amid the *associations* of heaven. It is the everlasting Sabbath: let us look in upon the assembly to which we expect to join ourselves in the sanctuary of the Church universal.

There we are communicants with all who, like ourselves, have been redeemed from the earth. While we loved God whom we had not seen we learned to love our brethren whom we had seen. The holy intimacies of life will there be renewed. Hearts which burned while fellow-believers talked along the way of their crucified Saviour, will experience rekindled ardor in together looking upon his exalted state. No distrust will there enter to cool the affection of the brotherhood. No suspicions of doctrinal unsoundness and no carnal ambitions will divide the general assembly of the triumphant Church into rival sections.

There will be no separate communions, and no contention for forms and modes. The partition-walls will be broken down, and hearts will blend in the burning of such love as angels feel.

The cord of caste will be broken, and national antipathies will be forgotten. The Barbarian and Scythian, the bond and free, the Hottentot and the child of civilization will together adore the wonders of the mercy which raised them from the spiritual degradation where they alike lay, and will mingle their voices in one choral exaltation of Him who is, without respect of persons, the Father and Redeemer of them all. The watchmen will lift up the voice together, and the intercession of Christ that we may be one, as he and the Father are one, will receive its fruition. The great and good of past ages, whose memory in the Church is like ointment poured forth, are all there. We shall sit down with Abraham, Isaac and Jacob, and the elders who obtained a good report—with saints of the New Testament, and glorious martyrs who have gone up in chariots of fire. All the Church, gone, living, and yet to live, will gather as one flock around the one Shepherd and Bishop of souls.

Angels will also be our associates there. The lowliest Christian will be the companion of those sons of God whose joyous shouts heralded the morning hour of earth. Those who have ascended from the unnoticed corners of the world, neglected and scorned by men, will stand by the side of Gabriel in the palace of the Great King. What a scene for Christian anticipation—to unite in angelic worship—to come into eternal intimacy with the noblest and holiest beings below God!

With the noblest and holiest beings *below* God—is that all? Nay, wondrous, wondrous grace! hope is taught to vault up to an infinity beyond this. We expect an eternal intimacy with the noblest and holiest of all—the Triune Father, Son and Holy Ghost. We shall sit down with Christ in his throne, and we shall be ever with the Lord. "They are before the throne of God, and serve him day and night in his temple, and he that sitteth on the throne shall dwell among them;" "The tabernacle of God is with men, and he will dwell with them, and they shall be his people, and God himself shall be with them, and be their God."

It seems too much, but the intercession of our Advocate makes it sure: "Father, *I will* that they also whom thou hast given me be with me where I am, that they may behold my glory which thou hast given me." In this world our richest foretastes of heaven are the approaches, distant though they be, which we make toward God. This is the comfort of warm-hearted prayer—the drawing near to him in whose presence there is fullness of joy. Whatever brings the soul near to God purifies its character and exalts its happiness. What will it then be to stand before his throne or to sit down with Christ, no more a stranger, but in the household home of his family?

"Think then," says Mr. Baxter, in his *Dying Thoughts*—"think, O my soul, what life thou shalt live for ever, in the presence and bosom of infinite and eternal Love! He now shineth on me by the sun, and on my soul by the Sun of Righteousness, but it is as through the crevices of my darksome habitation; but then he will shine on me and in me openly, and with the fullest streams and beams of love. Study this heavenly work of love, O my soul! It is only love that can understand it. Here the will has its taste. What can poor carnal worldlings know of glorious love who study it without love?"

These are the gatherings of heaven; this is the general assembly in the presence of its Head. Forgiven sinners are brought with songs to Zion, and there they worship with the innumerable company of angels. Jehovah is there, and there his glory is seen and felt as it shines in the face of Jesus. The joy of God is the joy of all, and the love which God *is* glows in every breast around. We have no human language for speaking of such fellowship, and no earthly things by which to illustrate it. This world is too poor to produce them. If the writer and reader may hereafter stand on the mountain of Zion, and together

> "Range the sweet plains on the banks of the river,
> And sing of salvation for ever and ever,"

we shall discourse of our celestial associations in terms befitting the theme.

Finally—heaven is *eternal*. What Christian, in his transient and uncertain hours of devotion, has not clung fondly to the thought that

> "There the assembly ne'er breaks up,
> The Sabbath ne'er shall end?"

Our Sabbaths on earth come and depart. Their holy quiet is followed by a week of worldly turmoil. We would fain be still with God, but the demands of the world upon our care are imperative. From the solemn sanctuary we must pass to the noisy street; from our altars of heavenly communion we must turn to intercourse with the vain world; from the mount of privilege we must descend to the cheerless deserts where few of the healing waters flow. We love the hours when we are allowed to put the world aside and dwell in undisturbed nearness to God, and we would gladly lay hold of the wheels of time and check the speed with which they are borne away; but they will go.

To the soul, feeling that a day with God is better than a thousand with the world, what bliss attends the reflection that the worship of the upper sanctuary is everlasting! Rob the saints in glory of that prospect, and every song of heaven would be changed into a wail of anguish. Give them to understand that at some period—no matter though it be millions of years remote—their bliss will terminate and their existence end, and every mansion and bower of paradise would be hung with funeral drapery. But no such fear will ever disturb a heart there. Everything in heaven is immortal. Its exemptions, its employments, its society, its Redeemer and King are all eternal. Our inheritance is incorruptible, and never fades away: "They shall reign for ever and ever."

What thoughts cluster around the word *Eternity!* Under the present darkness of our minds the conception is almost oppressive. We measure duration by days and years, and even in imagination we can follow it no farther than our arithmetic will number its periods. Still away onward, far beyond the stretch of our computation or thought, eternity rolls on. Worlds faint in the race and expire. Planetary systems are worn out by the friction of ages of revolving, and are lost in the regions of space. Still away onward, Time, fresh as in the morning of creation, is girding himself for a race without a goal.

Under such conceptions who can speak to creatures like ourselves, yet on earth, of eternal love, eternal holiness, eternal heaven? When we reflect that so much peace, joy and glory is to become an eternal reward, it seems like pouring into a cup which is already running over. Description is soon exhausted, but our musings linger on the thought that we shall be ever with the Lord. *Ever, ever* with the Lord!

Child of the skies! let thy spirit hasten

homeward. Tempests are gathering, and the nights of earth are dark and fearful. There "thy sun shall no more go down, neither shall thy moon withdraw itself; for the Lord shall be thine everlasting light, and the days of thy mourning shall be ended."

www.ingramcontent.com/pod-product-compliance
Lightning Source LLC
LaVergne TN
LVHW010218110826
845151LV00004B/1122

* 9 7 8 1 4 2 5 5 2 8 0 6 5 *